Virgo

Virgo

AUGUST 24–SEPTEMBER 23

Your Sun-and-Moon Guide
to Love and Life

Ronnie Dreyer

Ariel Books

**Andrews McMeel
Publishing**

Kansas City

For information write Andrews McMeel Publishing, an Andrews McMeel Universal company, 4520 Main Street, Kansas City, Missouri 64111.

www.andrewsmcmeel.com

Interior artwork by Robyn Officer

ISBN: 0-8362-3567-3

Library of Congress Catalog Card Number: 97-71534

$\mathcal{C}$ontents

Contents

Contents

Contents

Virgo

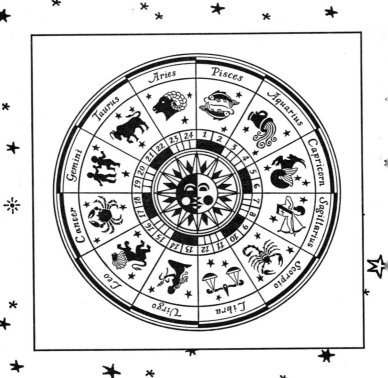

Introduction

Now, *you ask, might* astrology make a difference in your life, in your mental, emotional, and spiritual growth? Of course, there is no single answer to this question, for the responses are as diverse as humanity itself. Some of us may wish to dabble, enjoying astrology as we would a new hobby; have some fun; check out our sign and the signs of our friends, lovers, and children; and muse over the romantic possibilities of various combinations. What, for example, are the chances that a Libra man and a Pisces woman would hit it off? Others of us might wish to embark on a lifelong adventure, plumbing the depths of esoteric wisdom and emerging with startling new revelations about ourselves and our lives. Whatever your interest, you will find that astrology has something for everyone.

Astrology, which began as a search for a pattern in the cosmos, is based on the relationship between the infinitely large and the infinitely small, between the macrocosm—primarily our solar system, with its Sun, Moon, and planets, but also the fixed stars beyond—and the microcosm, the mysterious individual personality. In other words, astrology is the study of how celestial bodies influence the Earth and affect the human beings who dwell here.

In this regard, it's important to understand that astrology deals with symbols. The signs of the zodiac represent powerful forces, profound energies of the mind, heart, and soul. These energies are expressed in our personal horoscope, or birth chart, which describes the position of the heavens at our moment of birth and therefore portrays our unique personalities, our likes and dislikes, our strengths and weaknesses, our hopes and fears.

A horoscope is not, however, a simple reading of the future, a trip to the fortune-teller. You might want to consider your horoscope as a kind of map, indicating, say, the model of car you are driving, the condition of its motor, the state of the road (which may be bumpy in some places and smooth in others), and the variety of spiritual and emotional terrain you are likely to encounter during your life's journey. Perhaps the motor needs a tune-up; perhaps two roads pass through a particular stretch of wilderness, one road potholed and poor, the other sure and clear; perhaps just off the beaten path lies a great marvel you would miss if you didn't know it was there. What you do with the map astrology provides is up to you: You are free to choose, free to act as you will, free to make the most of your life—and, too, free to have plenty of fun along the way.

A Brief History

Long ago, men and women looked up into the starry night sky and wondered what it was and what effect it had on their lives. From that first primordial inquiry, astrology was born. No one quite knows how far back astrology's oral tradition extends; its first appearance in recorded history dates to 2500 B.C. in ancient Mesopotamia, where it was believed that the heavenly bodies were great gods with powers to influence the course of human affairs. Those early astrologers began to observe the heavens carefully and keep systematic records of what they saw in the great glittering silence of the night sky. The royal family's astrological counselors advised them on how to rule; early in its history, astrology was considered the "royal art."

The ancient Greeks already boasted

an ample pantheon of gods by the time their astronomers began to use the new science of geometry to explain the workings of the heavens. The Greeks combined Mesopotamia's form of astrological divination with their own mythology and the new science of geometry, developing a personal astrology based on the zodiac—from the Greek *zodiakos kyklos*, or "circle of animals"—a belt extending nine degrees on either side of the ecliptic, the Sun's apparent annual path across the sky. The belt was divided into segments named after animals—the Ram, the Bull, the Crab—and set to correspond to certain dates of the year. The Greeks were thus able to use astrology to counsel individuals who were curious about the effect of the heavens on their lives; the art of reading personal horoscopes was born.

As one seer of the times said, speaking of the heavens, "There is no speech nor language where their voice is not heard." Astrology was incorporated into Roman culture and spread with the extension of the Roman Empire throughout Europe. With the rise of Christianity, astrology faced a challenge: After all, it seemed to suggest that humans were determined by the stars, rather than by the stars' creator, who also, according to emerging Christian theology, had granted humans free will. Generally, however, astrology was absorbed into Christian teachings and continued to flourish; witness the selection of an astrological date for Christmas. Like much of classical culture, astrology went into decline during the Middle Ages, emerging in the early Renaissance to occupy a privileged place in the world of learning; in the sixteenth and seventeenth centuries, it was embraced by the prominent astronomers

Tycho Brahe and Johannes Kepler and was taught as a science in Europe's great universities.

Eventually, the discoveries of modern science began to erode the widely held belief in astrology's absolute scientific veracity. In our times, though, astrology remains as popular as ever, as an alternative to scientific theory, and as a way for people to articulate the manifold richness of the self. Psychologist Carl

Jung noted that astrology "contains all the wisdom of antiquity"; for modern men and women in search of the soul, it holds perennial interest as an expression of the psyche's mysterious relationship to the myriad wonders of the universe.

The Heavens

An Overview

In astrology, the art of relating events on Earth to influences in the heavens, each celestial body exerts its own form of power, which is modified according to its geometric relationship with the others. The heavens are made up of several kinds of celestial bodies. First, of course, there is the solar system—the Sun, Moon, and planets. Beyond the solar system lies the infinity of fixed stars, so-called because, as opposed to the planets, which the ancients could observe moving across the sky, the stars were always in the same place. Your horoscope plots the placement of the celestial bodies at the time of your birth.

When we speak of the heavens in astrology, we often speak of the zodiac, an imaginary belt extending nine degrees on either side of the ecliptic, the apparent path of the Sun across the sky. (Remember that the zodiac was devised in antiquity, when it was believed that the Sun revolved around the Earth.) The zodiac is divided into twelve arcs, or constellations, of thirty degrees each. Each arc is accorded a name and associated with the dates during which the Sun made its annual passage through that region of the sky at the time the zodiac was first devised. Your sun sign, the most widely known of the many astrological signs, refers to the particular arc of the zodiac through which the Sun was passing at the time of your birth. (With the procession of the equinoxes, the solar path may not always correspond to the actual solar chart.) The zodiac belt also contains the orbits of the Moon and most of the planets.

The solar system, then, constitutes the most important influence on human affairs. In ancient times, it was believed that the planets had their own light (the Sun and Moon were considered planets). Only five planets—Mercury, Venus, Mars, Jupiter, and Saturn—were visible to the ancients; Uranus, Neptune, and Pluto have been discovered over the last two hundred years. The influence of each planet depends on its position in the zodiac and its relation to the other celestial bodies, including the fixed stars. While some astrologers maintain that the planets are primarily refractors of influences from the more distant stars, most believe that each planet, along with the Sun and Moon, has its own characteristics that uniquely influence us—how we think, feel, and act. This influence can be positive and constructive or negative and self-destructive. Ultimately, the planets' disposition in your chart is a way of expressing various possibilities, which you can interpret and act upon as you choose.

The Solar System

Most astrologers
agree that the primary

influences come from within our own solar system—the Sun, Moon, and planets. Each planet is said to rule over one or two signs of the zodiac and have sway over a particular part of the body. Over the centuries, each planet has come to represent or influence a different aspect of the personality.

The Sun, which rules Leo, represents the conscious, creative aspects of the self. In a chart, a well-placed, strong

Sun indicates a dignified, self-possessed, affectionate, and authoritative personality; a badly placed Sun can suggest an ostentatious and dictatorial nature. The Sun rules the heart. Solar types tend to be energetic (the Sun, after all, is our source of energy) and like to take on large-scale projects that make good use of their many talents. They often make excellent top-level executives.

On the other hand, the Moon,

which rules over zodiacal Cancer, represents the imagination and is often linked by astrologers with the unconscious, hidden part of humans. In a chart, a prominent Moon usually indicates a sensitive and vulnerable nature, which can often be quite delightful; a badly placed Moon, however, can suggest an unhealthy and even dangerous self-absorption. In terms of the body, the Moon rules over the breasts. Lunarians are adaptable and often protective; perfectly capable of enjoying the delights of a quiet life at home, many also seek the public spotlight.

Mercury, the smallest planet and the one closest to the Sun, rules Gemini and Virgo. Like the Roman messenger of the gods whose name it shares, Mercury represents communication, speech, and wit, along with an often changeable disposition. Mercurians tend to be sensitive to their environment; they epitomize verbal and written expression and are often journalists and writers.

Venus, the most brilliant planet, rules Taurus and Libra; the planet of love, it governs the higher emotions, physical beauty, creativity, sex appeal, and sensual experience in all its many forms. It has rule over the throat. Venusians love beauty and art; they can at times be concerned with the surface of things, allowing image to become everything.

Mars, the planet that physically most resembles Earth, rules over Aries; representing the physical side of life, it combines with Venus to influence our sex drive. In a chart, Mars means courage, confidence, and the aggressive urges—the result-oriented ability to take on a project and get it done. In terms of the body, Mars has sway over the sex organs, particularly for men.

Jupiter, the largest planet in the solar

system, rules Sagittarius and represents the more profound realms of thinking and mental life, as well as the depths of the spirit. Jupiter suggests generosity, loyalty, success, and steady, solid growth. In terms of the body, it has sway over the thighs, liver, and blood. Jupiterians tend to be thoughtful, even philosophical, with plenty of social skills and an adventurous love of travel; Jupiter women are often strikingly beautiful.

Saturn, the farthest from Earth of the traditional planets, represents fears, uncertainties, and materialistic concerns. It can indicate practicality, patience, and honesty, although, if badly placed in a chart, Saturn can also suggest a deep fear of life. It governs the human skeleton, emphasizing this planet's role in providing structure and control; Saturnians tend to make good accountants and bureaucrats.

Uranus, discovered in the eighteenth century, rules Aquarius. Often representing change, even upheaval, it can be a beneficent influence, representing the kind of brilliant flash of insight that can instigate bold new ways of thinking. Yet its independent and rebellious nature can pose problems, when liberty turns to license and at times even to crime.

Neptune, discovered in the mid-nineteenth century, has rule over Pisces.

On its beneficent side, it can represent idealism, art, and imagination; its connection with the sea (Neptune was the Roman god of the ocean) indicates its tendency to affect the unconscious aspects of the psyche. This can bring great power; it can also, however, suggest a preference to dream rather than act.

Pluto, discovered in 1930, now rules Scorpio. The planet farthest from the Sun, Pluto often represents the dark forces of desire and instinct that seek dissolution of the self within the great cosmos. While there are dangers here, there is as well the potential for profound healing.

The Signs of the Zodiac

W
hen we speak
of the signs of the zodiac,

we refer to the twelve thirty-degree arcs of the sky into which the zodiac is divided. Each sign is represented by an image derived from ancient descriptions of the constellations; however, the astrological signs of the zodiac should not be confused with the actual constellations whose names they sometimes share. The most important signs are the sun signs, by which is meant the particular zone of the sky through which the Sun was passing at the time of someone's birth.

The signs of the zodiac are as follows:

Aries (the Ram), March 21–April 20

Taurus (the Bull), April 21–May 21

Gemini (the Twins), May 22–June 21

Cancer (the Crab), June 22–July 23

Leo (the Lion), July 24–August 23

Virgo (the Virgin), August 24–September 23

Libra (the Scales), September 24–October 23

Scorpio (the Scorpion), October 24–November 22

Sagittarius (the Archer), November 23–December 21

Capricorn (the Goat), December 22–January 20

Aquarius (the Water Bearer), January 21–February 19

Pisces (the Fish), February 20–March 20

The zodiacal signs are also symbols for the great forces that lie deeply within our minds, hearts, and souls and exist in different combinations from one person to the next. Each sign is associated with a different part of the body. In total, the twelve signs express all that we are as humans. The signs are said to be composed of four different elements and three different qualities.

The Four
Elements

T*he four elements* through which the twelve signs of the zodiac are expressed are fire, earth, air, and water. For the Greeks, they were the fundamental substances of the universe. In astrology, these elements are also spiritual and symbolic; they are expressed in connection with three different qualities—cardinal, fixed, and mutable. Each element has one cardinal sign, one fixed sign, and one mutable sign; and each quality is expressed through each element, as in the chart that follows:

	Cardinal	*Fixed*	*Mutable*
Fire	Aries	Leo	Sagittarius
Earth	Capricorn	Taurus	Virgo
Air	Libra	Aquarius	Gemini
Water	Cancer	Scorpio	Pisces

In addition, the four elements, which are restless and in conflict with one another, are often said to be bound together by a mysterious, invisible fifth element, known as the "quintessence," which is responsible for maintaining the often tenuous unity of all things on Earth.

Fire Signs

*T*he fire element, expressed
through Aries, Leo, and Sagittarius, is
profoundly linked to the spirit. Fire is a
powerful elemental force; impulsive,

iconoclastic, and warm, the fire signs are eternally seeking expression. If not regulated in some way, however, fire can turn destructive, burning out of control.

Aries—outgoing, idealistic, enthusiastic—requires great freedom in order to achieve its maximum sense of self. Often brimming with confidence, the Aries type tends to act impulsively and not always with proper concern for what other people may think or feel. This spontaneity can be tremendously attractive, but it can at times become selfish and over-bearing.

Leo, on the other hand, while also possessing a deep need for freedom, tends to be much more sensitive to others. Given to the exuberant and flamboyant, Leo's creativity is frequently expressed through art and drama. Self-reliant and generally optimistic, the Leo nature also has a vein of altruism; Leos can, though, at times be a bit vain.

Sagittarius, the mutable fire sign, is characterized by qualities of profound yearning and aspiration. Open, honest, and generous, Sagittarians tend to be hungry for growth and expansion. They are very independent—sometimes to a fault—and are often great seekers, for whom the journey is more important than the destination.

Earth Signs

*T*he earth element, expressed through Taurus, Virgo, and Capricorn, is deeply connected to physical things. Generally, it reflects the practical, down-to-earth side of human nature. It is also said to be an incarnating principle by which spirituality takes on form. Not surprisingly, the earth and water elements enjoy a close relationship, with earth stabilizing water and water making the arid earth fertile.

Taurus, the fixed earth sign, tends toward the sedentary. Slow, practical, and conservative, a person born under Taurus will likely evidence an unspectacular, solid determination. Taurus is receptive to the joys of a gentle, stable existence—a regular paycheck, a nice house, warm relationships, a comfortable routine. When frustrated or threatened, however, the Taurus nature can turn possessive and jealous.

Virgo, the mutable earth element, is drawn toward ephemeral things, engrossed in "what is past, or passing, or to come." Intellectual, elegant, intelligent, and methodical, Virgo is driven to seek the clarity of understanding. When subjected to intense stress, though, Virgo can become hypercritical and a bit of a nag.

Capricorn, the cardinal earth element, is dependable, solid, trustworthy, and prudent. The Capricorn nature will plow steadily ahead, connected to its roots and clear about what it wishes to achieve in life. Yet in stressful situations Capricorn can become selfish and rigid.

Air Signs

The air element, expressed through Gemini, Libra, and Aquarius, has long been associated with thought, dating back to the ancient concept that thinking is the process by which humans take in ideas from the world around them, much as they take in air through breathing. All three air signs generally are dominated by tendencies toward restlessness; they are also known as the nervous signs. However, they are each unique.

Gemini is particularly volatile, a whirlwind constantly blowing in many directions. The Gemini nature is inventive, alert, and communicative, but Geminis can at times become unstable and wild, even hysterical.

Libra is like a strong wind that blows purposefully in a single direction. Its influence is elegant and orderly. Libras tend to be perceptive and affectionate, sensitive to others and aware of their needs, although in excess a Libra nature can be impractical and a bit lazy.

Aquarius, the calmest air sign, is associated with water as well as air; it represents spiritual knowledge, creativity, and freedom. The Aquarian nature tends toward the rational and places great value on freedom, sometimes sacrificing the future in the name of rebellion.

Water Signs

The water element, expressed through Cancer, Pisces, and Scorpio, represents the fluidity, spirituality, and sensitivity in our nature. Often emotional, sometimes to the point of instability, the water element needs to find some kind of container in order to realize its true potential.

Cancer, represented by the Crab, is emotional, imaginative, and romantic; it can also be very cautious. There is something gentle and shy about the Cancer nature; afraid of being hurt, it is sometimes slow to come out of—and quick to return to—its shell. Such vulnerability can be deeply touching; in excess, however, it can turn moody and self-absorbed.

Scorpio, the most self-confident of the water signs, is masterful, shrewd, and determined. Possessed of strong desires, Scorpio types are not easily dissuaded from pursuing their goals. In doing so, they can be forceful and inspirational; yet when threatened, they can exhibit a violent streak, and when thwarted they can turn sarcastic and cruel.

Emotional and highly intuitive Pisces is also quick to retreat from the slings and arrows of life. Often this is because the Pisces nature is so sensitive to the emotional needs of others that it will sometimes forget its own interests and need to seek temporary refuge, in order to find its own center again. It has to be careful, though, not to fall into the trap of self-pity.

The Three Qualities

There are three qualities, or modes of expression, through which each of the four elements finds expression in the twelve signs of the zodiac: cardinality, fixity, and mutability.

The qualities are another way of expressing features the different signs share; all
four fixed signs, for example, will have
certain features in common, in that they
will tend to be more stable than the mutable signs within their same element.
This may seem complicated, but the
basic principle is actually pretty simple.

The cardinal quality serves as the
origin of action, the wellspring of energy
that gets things done in the world. It's the

"mover and shaker" personality—active, outward-looking, more geared to "doing" than to "being." The four cardinal signs are Aries, Cancer, Libra, and Capricorn; each is self-assertive, but in a unique way. Capricorn, the earth cardinal sign, tends to take solid, dependable action that is often geared toward material success, while Aries, the fire sign, often acts in a much more spontaneous, even impulsive, way. Libra, the air sign, is particularly assertive on the intellectual level, quick to advance its ideas and defend them when they are questioned. Cancer, the water sign, tends toward caution and often will act prudently.

The fixed quality serves to temper movement; it functions as an impediment, an often valuable check on the rampant free flow of energy. Sometimes expressed as "will," the fixed signs—Taurus, Leo, Scorpio, and Aquarius—are likely to be resistant to change and appreciate tradition and known, sure values. Taurus, the earth sign, is the most sedentary of all, with deep, latent powers and a clear preference for staying in one place. Leo, the fire sign, embodies a sustained emotional warmth and loyalty that is not likely to change over time. With Scorpio, the water sign, power takes on a more fluid form, exhibiting an unshakable self-confidence that remains firm in the face of adversity. Aquarius, meanwhile, is the most cool and composed of the air signs; Aquarians trust rational thinking and extend deep roots into the ideas they hold and the places where they live.

The mutable quality embodies the principles of flexibility and adaptability. The mutable signs—Gemini, Virgo, Sagittarius, and Pisces—could be said to combine aspects of cardinal impulsiveness with those of the unyielding fixed temperament. Gemini, the mutable air sign, is particularly given to surprising transformations of the self; you think you know a Gemini, and then, *presto!* you realize that you knew only one side of the person's nature. Virgo, the earth sign, is often irresistibly drawn toward the shifting play of ideas and thought. For Sagittarius, the fire sign, change often equals growth; driven to expand, the Sagittarian nature seems eternally questing after something new. Pisces, the water sign, often embodies the fluid, changing character of the emotions; sensitive to the smallest alterations of feelings, it can ride the waves of emotional life like a skilled surfer.

Virgo
An Introduction

This mutable earth sign,

the sixth of the zodiac, is symbolized by a gentle maiden holding a sheaf of harvested corn. Those born under this sign are the most kindhearted, reliable, and efficient people in existence: You are sensitive, and highly self-conscious about everything you do. You are a willing and ultradiligent worker whose keen intellect, clever wit, and verbal fluidity will always come to your aid; although you may never be entirely at ease speaking in public, you can make appointments, sell your wares, and communicate easily with anyone you like through the magic of the telephone or computer screen.

But you are also hypercritical, both of yourself and others, and everything you do is meticulously thought out, with a careful eye cast towards the future. You take it for granted that if everything is executed according to your methodical plan of action, happy endings will inevitably result; yet anything that falls short of perfection is a failure in your eyes. Others would crow at your accomplishments; you can only nitpick. This attitude can be dangerous, especially if you extend your obsession with flawlessness to family and friends. You may be a wonderful and loyal confidante who can be trusted with the darkest of secrets, but the unsolicited advice you offer in the name of "improvement" can be impertinent, or even insulting. The best of friendships can end at the snap of the fingers. Beware of ulcers. Indeed, the Virgo glyph can be said to resemble the coil-shaped large intestines!

Myths
and
Legends

Throughout the folklore of innumerable

cultures, the fertility goddess is depicted as a benevolent, compassionate helpmate who uses her unlimited powers to fertilize the earth. She is also on a quest, and her indefatigable search for a child, sibling, or lover who has been abducted to the underworld displays all the Virgin traits of endless devotion, patience, allegiance, and love.

Separated from her loved one, the heartbroken goddess cannot bear to water the earth, which results in a dry and unproductive summer. Once the two are reunited, however, the rainy season ensues, and grain can once again be planted, harvested, and distributed to her people. The Sumerian Inanna and her son/lover, Dumuzi; the Egyptian Isis and her brother, Osiris; the Phoenician Astarte and her lover, Baal, are famous examples of fertility deities whose separations and reunions mark the difference between sterile and fruitful seasons.

But perhaps the best-known tale involves Demeter (Ceres in the Roman version), the Greco-Roman goddess of grain whose daughter Persephone (Proserpine) is abducted to the underworld by its lord, Hades (Pluto). Demeter is generally portrayed either with her daughter on her lap or holding a sheaf of corn; in both cases she demonstrates fierce determination and ceaseless loyalty in assuring that Persephone, to whom she is eternally bound, is returned home safe and sound.

The story unfolds as Persephone innocently gathers a bouquet of flowers in the Eleusinian Fields. Suddenly, from out of nowhere, Hades swoops down upon the young girl with whom he is infatuated and abducts her to his home in the land of the dead. Demeter, devastated by the loss of her daughter, retreats to her temple and immediately stops watering the earth. With the support of her people, who fear starvation, Demeter mourns, performs rituals of purification, and prays for Persephone's safe return. (These rites are perhaps comparable to the disciplined diet and exercise regime that the devoted, compassionate, and benevolent Virgo practices on its road to perfection.)

Deeply concerned about his kingdom, Zeus, the king of the gods, sends

Hermes, the divine messenger, to mediate a compromise with Hades so that Persephone will spend three months in the underworld (the parched, inactive summer) and nine months with her mother in Greece. The harvest is celebrated; Demeter is praised, and fertility, devotion, and maternal love reign supreme.

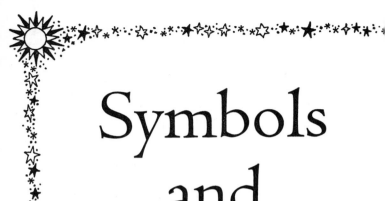

Symbols
and
Associations

Because the age
of Virgo (12,000-

10,000 B.C.) predates the written word, there is no accurate record of the motifs that define this era. It is interesting to note, however, that the age of Pisces, which is Virgo's polar opposite, is inundated with images of the Virgin, a primary symbol of Christianity, holding a newborn child in her arms.

Every zodiacal sign has a ruling planet and a detrimental planet, which are strengthened and weakened respectively when placed in that particular sign. Each planet is also exalted, at its strongest, or fallen, at its weakest, when placed in a specific sign. Mercury (named for the Roman messenger of the gods) rules Virgo, supplying communication skills, analytical abilities, and a keen intellect, but Neptune, the planet of impression-ability, fantasy, and spirituality, is detri-mental, or not very comfortable, there. Mercury is exalted in Virgo, whereas

Venus, the planet of love, beauty, and self-worth, is fallen in that same sign.

Virgos are *meticulous, helpful, gentle, humble, efficient, practical, reliable, intellectual, organized, logical, health-conscious, tender, sensual, kindhearted, judicious, dedicated, work-oriented,* and *service-minded.*

They are also *critical, nervous, high-strung, overly cautious, analytical, obsessive, worrisome, pessimistic, mean-spirited, sharp-tongued, absentminded, moralistic, nasty,* and *cold.*

Virgo archetypes are the helper, the analyst, the craftsman, and the critic. Professions include physical therapist, masseuse, nutritionist, social worker, counselor, secretary, administrator, writer, teacher, accountant, economist, chemist, and office worker.

Parts of the body ruled by Virgo include the intestines, bowels, gall bladder, and pancreas. Mercury governs the nervous system. Virgin countries include

Brazil, Turkey, and Switzerland. Jerusalem, Athens, Boston, and Paris are Virgo-ruled cities.

Colors associated with Virgo are blue and gray. If you were born between August 24 and August 31, your birthstone is peridot. If you were born between September 1 and September 23, your birthstone is sapphire. Other gems associated with Virgo are agate, sardonyx, marble, and jasper. The metals are nickel, copper, and quicksilver.

Plants ruled by Virgo include dandelion, valerian, skullcap, and woodbine. Flowers ruled by Virgo are pansies. Virgin foods include endive, millet, corn, wheat, barley, oats, rye, tomatoes, beets, lemons, celery, grapefruit, apples, cauliflower, oranges, milk, and figs. Herbs and spices are rosemary, pulsatilla, and motherwort.

Famous Virgo personalities include Yāsir Arafāt, Ingrid Bergman, Leonard

Bernstein, Jacqueline Bisset, Geraldine Ferraro, Greta Garbo, Julio Iglesias, Michael Jackson, Lyndon Baines Johnson, Ricki Lake, Sophia Loren, Regis Philbin, John Ritter, Charlie Sheen, Mother Teresa, Leo Tolstoy, Lily Tomlin, and Raquel Welch.

The Virgo motto is "Do unto others as you would have others do unto you."

Health
and
Physique

The Virgo type is
frequently characterized

by a high forehead, kind eyes, thin nose, well-formed mouth, pointed chin, and broad jawline. You are medium to tall in height, thin to average in weight, and usually very serious; and although you are not necessarily strong and robust, you will never be deterred by physical labor or fierce intellectual challenges. Indeed, working as long as it takes to get the job done is one of your hallmarks. You may appear cool and aloof at first, but in the end you will be best remembered for your willingness to offer help to those in need.

Because of your high-strung disposition and sensitive nervous system, you should avoid nicotine, caffeine, and anything else calculated to stimulate activity. Your talkative manner and upbeat personality cannot mask your innate pessimism or prevent you from internalizing rather than sharing your thoughts and

feelings with others; the stress and un-
necessary worry to which these habits
lead will tend to aggravate your already
sensitive digestive system and intestinal
tract. It is crucial that your diet include
plenty of fresh fruits and vegetables, sup-
plemented by the proper vitamins and
minerals, so that your body can function
consistently and at its best.

Every zodiacal sign corresponds to a
part of the human anatomy, so the horo-

scope can reveal which organs and areas of the body may be vulnerable and prone to illness. Your tendency to brood could predispose you to a nervous stomach, ulcers, constipation, or even, in extreme cases, gallstones and intestinal disorders like colitis and Crohn's disease. (Recent research has shown that ulcers may be bacterially induced, but the extent to which they are aggravated by emotional stress should not be underestimated.)

Yours is the most health-conscious sign of the zodiac, so you will stay physically fit through good diet, regular exercise, and plenty of fresh air. To avoid the nervousness and irritability that stimulate the butterflies in your stomach, you might also consider practicing meditation or other relaxation techniques like deep breathing, biofeedback, and positive visualization.

Most likely you are already a frequent customer at the local health food store, so next time you are there, ask about special teas—such as chamomile—that can soothe your upset stomach and help you relax.

Personality

Though you are
meticulous, unflinchingly

loyal, and amazingly productive, you are also as notorious for your idiosyncrasies as for your systematic habit of making everything fall neatly into place. Your verbal and communicative skills glitter when you go one-on-one, not only because you are truly interested in other people's plights but because you *listen*. You pay attention and have a sharp eye for detail, whereas other signs will wander; and what moves you the most, in the end, is the knowledge that you have, in some minute way, made a difference in someone else's life. For all this, however, you are always nervous, fidgety, and painfully aware of yourself in a room filled with people!

The contradictions continue because you can be the model employee and caregiver *to a fault:* Your damn-the-torpedoes dedication to finishing whatever you begin (whether personally or professionally) may cause you to recoil from socializing until your work is fully completed. The danger is that you will turn into a hermit or deny yourself the simple pleasures of life just because you haven't lived up to your exceedingly high (indeed unrealistic) standards. Severe perfectionist that you are, you will never be satisfied with anything you do, so you might as well relax, enjoy yourself, and learn to have a good time.

Your demure demeanor may lead

certain people to assume that you are submissive or weak. Others will go to the opposite extreme and find you cool, even hard-nosed, when you first meet. Instead, you are one of the most helpful, compassionate, and generous souls in the world, but there is no question that you can stop on a dime and turn unpleasantly critical; and your overdeveloped sense of logic and reason can make you appear devoid of imagination and able to see only what is straight before your eyes.

You do not trust easily and may even be suspicious of people who are overly gregarious and always upbeat. Once you decide that someone is genuine and not going to manipulate you or abuse your friendship, however, you will readily reverse your opinion and give absolutely everything you have to the relationship. And when you do finally let another person into your heart, you are one of the most devoted and compassionate friends—or lovers—anyone could hope to find.

Career

You have a powerful
need to serve; this, coupled

with your interest in physical and mental health, will attract you to medicine or related professions. A well-equipped and dedicated caregiver, you would hit your stride as a doctor, nurse, physical or occupational therapist, nutritionist, counselor, psychologist, or social worker. Your determination to achieve supreme physical and psychological balance could lead you to explore alternative therapies like acupuncture, massage, or homeopathy. You might even feel at home in a health-food store. Whether the path is traditional, holistic, or completely off the beaten track, however, you will seek out the method best suited to fulfill your quest for perfection. And even if you do not gravitate to a helping profession *per se*, your friends, family, and coworkers will probably view you as a medical authority nevertheless. This should surprise no one, since you constantly quote medical texts, suggest over-the-counter remedies, and offer health advice, whether solicited or not.

You are unlikely to establish your own business, but your extraordinary ability to organize files, hammer out details, analyze, and ultimately resolve any given problem would make you the best assistant or secretary anyone could possibly desire. No matter what your profession, you can single-handedly run an entire office.

The god of communication rules you, so verbal and written skills are second nature to you; and because you love few things more than taking an object apart and putting it back together again, you might easily become a successful mystery writer, crossword puzzle designer, researcher, editor, linguist, interpreter, or graphic artist. In somewhat different fields, your clarity and logic could serve you superbly as a mathematician, financial analyst, accountant, chemist, or, perhaps above all, teacher. Your obsession with details and order will make you the neatest and most meticulous member of the faculty, ever-present at meetings and always taking detailed notes. If you're an elementary school teacher, your classroom will run like a Swiss watch—and your students will have the best handwriting in the school. If you're a college professor, you will create detailed syllabi for your students and insist that they write cogent, well-thought-out papers.

You will give 100 percent no matter what you do and will be a valued coworker to your colleagues. You will exert every effort to reach the goals you have set for yourself, and many moons will pass before anyone even approaches your level of near-perfection.

Love
and
Marriage

W

When it comes to
love and marriage, you

would probably agree with the song that says, "You can't have one without the other." Others may indulge in passionate affairs without ever letting the dreaded "M" word cross their lips, but you will lay it on the line from the get-go. Your logical brain will see it very simply: Strumming guitars and hot air balloon rides are all well and good, but why should you waste time on someone whose cold feet will prevent a walk down the aisle? If your intense feelings are insufficiently reciprocated, there's hardly a point even to beginning.

But what really prevents you from falling head over heels is your gnawing and almost self-destructive urge toward perfection . . . which no shoes ever can fill. Are you looking for undying love with a knight in shining armor or a fair maid more virtuous than the saints? When you meet someone new, do you coldly appraise (and eventually reject) every physical attribute? And if your heart does not flutter, your breath does not catch, and bells fail to ring the first time around, are you doomed before you ever say hello? If you answered "yes" to any of the above, you had better reevaluate—or decide to go live in a cave.

If true love is truly what you are after, you will have to get beyond first impressions, which are frequently shallow and very rarely ideal. If you can manage to live with the facial features and style of dress presented, you can then perhaps take a peek at the mind and the soul. Who knows what will happen after that? What matters most in the end is that you have a loving mate and intimate companion with whom you can share your hopes, dreams, worries, and fears as you negotiate together the byways of life.

Although you will be a tremendously supportive, devoted, and sympathetic partner, there still will be times when you are critical, cold, and aloof. You will find it difficult, if not impossible, to veer completely from your irritable moods, but if you can become more accepting of your imperfections, you will not only open your own heart, but will offer your lifelong mate the same friendship, understanding, and compassion that you extend to everyone else.

Home and Family

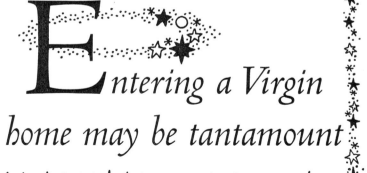

Entering a Virgin home may be tantamount

to walking into an enchanted palace in which every object glitters. Your household is so meticulous and tidy, indeed (a place for everything, and everything in its place), that the face on the dishes may actually smile back!

Whoever shares your life should not be fooled, however, by the Mary Poppins image you work so diligently to portray. You have a bit of a dark side, which may strike terror into the faint of heart because sooner or later all of those pieces of paper and other collectibles that you have so neatly placed in drawers, closets, and cupboards will spill out and show the world (or at least your family) what a pack rat you are. It is not that you are a fraud, exactly, but you would like the world to think you are perfect. You would like to *be* perfect, in fact, though you always feel you fall short; and however harsh you may be to others, you are twice as critical of yourself. If you forget to pick up the dry cleaning, for example, you berate yourself for half an hour.

You are one of those super beings who firmly believe you can be successful at home, work, *and* play—and if anyone can actually pull off that trifecta, it will probably be you. A little hard work never killed anyone, after all, and in any case you require less sleep than most other mortals, so there are more waking hours to your day. And although you may choose to work outside the home, you will nevertheless exert every fiber of your being to care for your family. You just plan every hour of your day and stick to your strict schedule in order to complete all your tasks.

You must be careful, however, not to pass your relentless quest for perfection onto your offspring. Your greatest gift to your children is precisely what you extend to colleagues and friends: availability at all times to listen and guide. Guiding them, however, does not mean critiquing their magic marker drawing and making suggestions for improvements! You are a wonderfully patient teacher, and your children will be among the earliest readers in school, but remember that they are *children*, so don't be disappointed if they want to run outside long before their lessons are completed.

If you allow them to mature at their own pace, you will see yourself reflected in the purposeful lifestyles they eventually embark upon. And nothing, in the end, will fill you with greater joy than knowing that your tireless efforts have been rewarded.

Virgo in Love

Critics say you haven't a passionate bone in your body, but the truth is simply that your particular brand of love and romance is not as richly tinged with fantasy (or lucre) as that of most other signs. It doesn't bother you in the least if you are not showered with lavish gifts on your anniversary or birthday;

but you *may* become upset if the one you love spends extravagantly when you can least afford it.

Glittering trinkets mean little to you, and you are far too clever and committed to the truth to fall for honeyed words alone. What counts, for you, is honoring the sentiment of a very special day. If the person of your dreams recalls what made you cry one afternoon, or recounts a little anecdote you once blurted out in passing, it will exhilarate and thrill you as much as a diamond ring would please most other people. In that very moment, as silly as it seems, you will know that the person you desire loves you enough to be interested in—and to remember—everything you say.

Spending time together, sharing your deepest thoughts, awakening your most hidden pleasures and senses—these, to you, are the aphrodisiacs that matter. And if promises of love go hand-in-hand with viable plans for a future together, then the modest, critical, and idealistic Virgin will suddenly shed its clothes and emerge with the sensual appetite of a wolf—one who has been wandering through the forest for weeks on end.

Virgo with Aries

MARCH 21–APRIL 20

Aries is dashing, daring, and highly abrasive; you are shy, sensitive, and ultracritical. The Ram longs for a life of exciting challenges and hurdles to overcome; you crave a dignified existence of perfect order and calm. You, perhaps, may be the greatest challenge the Ram will face. The two of you are as close as night and day, and if you jumped into this affair, you would both be taking the chance of a lifetime. But great things can come of great risks.

To begin with, you will find more excitement with the Ram than you ever realized existed. This ceaselessly active fire sign lives for exhilaration: crashing down the ski slopes, crashing against the white-water waves, crashing the most chic party in town. Your idea of thrills and chills is spending the evening curled up with a good murder mystery. You will now be invited to go out and *live;* and although you may initially react with terror at the idea, you should consider it carefully (how else do you do anything?) and then give it a whirl.

Of course you will want time to analyze every conceivable ramification, and fanatically impatient Aries will chomp at the bit with every wasted second that goes by. You will have to capitulate before you're quite ready, and even then, if you tarry too long, your mate will zip off to greener—and faster—pastures. This will be the paradigm of your life together . . . and would it really be so bad? Would it kill you to ponder a little less and arrive at your decisions a tad more speedily?

Would it tarnish you forever to scream a little more? You'll find out if you spend time with the Ram. Life with the Ram will be a bit dizzying, and it will make your Virginal cheeks flushed with excitement. Before you realize it, you'll be having lots of fun with Aries.

All is not always fun and games with the Aries, however. The Ram's volatile temper can flare at a moment's notice, and then a towering rage might ensue;

you merely worry and keep all your uglier emotions bottled up neatly inside. When annoyed, you pout and sulk; you may be in a bad mood for days before Aries notices. For the Ram, this will not do; your new partner can open up some healthy avenues of release for you. You, at the same time, might suggest a few ways of toning down your terribly excitable Ram.

Both of you will benefit from your dramatic give-and-take. Aries, notorious for never keeping track of time, might actually be grateful to you for providing the organization it so desperately needs. Unless it is reminded to slow down and take a break, the Ram will skip meals or even sleep. And when it finally does hear its stomach rumbling, it will rush into a fast-food dive simply because it has time for nothing else.

You, with your obsessive regard for health and proper diet, will change all

that and save Aries from an early grave—
if you can entice your love to spend fewer
hours at the local greasy spoon diner and
more of them at home. Both of you are
consumed with keeping your bodies in
shape (to you, it's work, and to Aries, it's
play), so perhaps you should gently remind the Ram how much you enjoy ex-
pending energy late at night. That is a
game of athletics that both of you will
greatly enjoy, and afterward, the Ram

161

may gladly allow you to organize the rest of your lives. Yes, this relationship can be a challenge to both of you, but if you work out your differences early and re-member always to compromise, you both will find yourselves as satisfied as you've been in years.

Virgo with Taurus

APRIL 21–MAY 21

Stable, practical, and lazy Taurus could be just what the doctor ordered to sedate your overactive mind and calm your severely frayed nerves.

This fixed earth sign is every bit as practical and sensible as you are, but temperamentally you stand in opposite corners of the ring. Whereas you are high-strung, the Bull is almost unflappably serene. Whereas you get everything done weeks before it is due, the Bull waits and lingers and crawls along until you start to pull out your hair. You fret; the Bull dozes. You want ceaselessly to improve your mind; the Bull's idea of bliss is to lie on the couch and watch TV. Few signs will frustrate you more. Few signs are as lovable.

Though Taurus will arouse your ire no end, it will also provide a bulky cushion to sink into after you have hit the proverbial roof . . . and "bulky" is indeed the word. You both may be earthy and sensual creatures, but your key word, "moderation," is unlisted in the Taurean lexicon. Take a glance at the heavenly smile on the Bull's face after it has downed a hearty gourmet meal followed by a rich, creamy dessert, and you will begin to understand. Only when Taurus lets out yet another notch on its belt will it finally cave in to vanity and beg you for support. You will give it gladly—helping to improve others is your favorite role— and you can teach the Bull how to be sated without stuffing its face. But you must do it with kindness and without your superior lectures. Offer Taurus friendship and love instead of cool, stern advice, and it will go to the ends of the earth to please you. Start giving orders, however, and the Bull will see red. Then its legendary stubbornness will kick in, and then it may storm its way out the door. But Taurus will not initiate arguments, so your happiness is in your hands.

So is your financial future, and the

two of you have an excellent formula for accumulating assets. Both of you are pragmatic; both of you respect money. Taurus is used to bailing others out of debt, and you would never allow yourself to get into it. People trust and will listen to you both, so you could dispense advice in almost any field and have a steady stream of clients knocking at your door. The only drawback is that neither of you is noted for an excess of get-up-and-go, so although you might love helping others, you still could feel overwhelmed at the idea of being at the world's (or anyone's) beck and call.

That is when you will lock up the house, gas up the car, and head for the secluded hills. When you finally reach a remote destination that suits both your critical eye and Taurus's need to relax, your earthy natures will have the opportunity to come together, blossom, and grow. You have helped the Bull see the folly of its ways by day; now let Taurus calm your sleepless nerves by night.

Virgo with Gemini

MAY 22–JUNE 21

Gemini is symbolized

by the Twins, who are impossible to nail
down: outgoing one moment but moody
the next, voluble and hyperkinetically

driven but also shallow and even afraid of emotion. This mutable air sign, like you, is ruled by Mercury, the fleet-footed messenger of the gods; and because both of your nervous systems will be running on empty much of the time, will either of you ever slow down long enough to listen to what the other has to say?

Before you shake your head, you might *try* listening to the Twins. You might even find that you enjoy it. Gemini could then return the favor by pulling you effort-lessly out of your pessimistic mode. The Twins will do almost anything for a laugh, and even you need to smile once in a while. And both of you like to let your minds ramble in a thousand different directions, so inevitably you are bound to hook up now and then. And since neither has an at-tention span worth discussing, you may well forget all about your disagreements al-most as soon as they crop up.

The problem is that they will crop up continually. The Twins will procrastinate forever if they possibly can; you like to act with quick precision and dispatch. The Twins can scarcely plan a trip to the front door; you need a schedule in hand before you can even consider waking up. The Twins like to gallivant throughout the wee small hours; you will be fast asleep when the night is still young. You like to wake at the crack of dawn, eat breakfast, and take a brisk early-morning walk; by then the Twins are dead to the world. When will you even have the opportunity to argue?

Gemini cherishes its freedom more than anything else in the world, so perhaps it would be wise to consider a part-time relationship—which could work out a great deal better than you think. The Twins can hop from interest to interest (going to the movies with an eclectic group of friends, traveling the information superhighway until the electronic cows come home), whereas you can figure out the best way to stay healthy and fit. With your extroverted Gemini out of the house, you can enjoy your quiet time alone: reading, rearranging, redecorating. The Twins could care less about cushions and curtains, so you, too, will have all the freedom you need—or desire. And that can have its charms.

And now that you have earned each other's respect, and perhaps begun to pine for each other's company, you can look forward to those times when you will chatter away (or engage in other activities) long into the night. You may have to stay up a little later, and Gemini rise a little earlier, but you both will agree that communication, of every sort, is the thing. If you can allocate the necessary time to talk, this relationship will survive

as long as each of you listens. And if you can work out a mutual bedtime on top of it, so much the better, indeed.

Virgo with Cancer

Y*ou and Cancer are* the great helpers of the zodiac: kind-hearted, maternal, the first on the scene when anyone needs aid. No others give of themselves so freely, yet you are also the most reserved and bashful signs in existence—and, perhaps, the most contradictory.

Along with your tender diligence comes an unpleasant tendency to criticize, and at times you can be so caustic and cruel that even your closest friends may recoil. And Cancer? This cardinal water sign is as wayward and changeable as the oceans: all smothering affection one minute and brutal withdrawal the next. The Crab, when threatened or hurt, draws into its shell and may never emerge again; and because it is so ultrasensitive, it can be threatened or hurt very easily. Your casual scorn and superiority are ill-calculated to put this crustacean at ease.

Cancer is all emotion: It communicates everything through its feelings, which change as often and tempestuously as the crashing waves. You are all mind, and when you want to, you could freeze an iceberg. If you freeze each other out when you don't get your way, what can possibly hold you together?

For starters, you are the two most family-minded signs in the heavens. And for all your potential bitterness, you are also the most receptive to another's pain. In many respects, the world would be a better place if there were more Virgins and Crabs to fill it. You are not Aquarian idealists, so you will never march on the White House or picket city hall; your service consists of a shoulder to lean on, an ear to listen, and advice that flows without provocation or axes to grind. Among family, friends, and neighbors, your house may buzz from morning till night, but hospitality is what you are famous for, and proudest of. Yet if the two of you are always engrossed in helping others in need, you could wind up ignoring each other. And the fact remains that for all of your considerable differences, you also have a great deal in common that few other signs share.

You are both gratified by things that many would consider dull. Quiet evenings at home sharing the preparation of a lavish meal, watching an old black-and-white weepie in the comfort of your bed, and giving each other your simple, undivided attention would strike both of you as heaven on earth. You also, for all of your ability to wound when pushed, will go out of your ways to avoid confrontation; and if you can manage to carve out any détente at all, you will probably last longer than most other couples.

If that strikes you as worth aiming for, then all you need to do is tell the Crab, who will delight in the simplest pleasures and loyalty, how much it is needed and loved. Once its many insecurities are put to rest, Cancer will cater to your own. Those pincers, once they grab hold, will never let go, and you will have a ferociously dedicated partner for the rest of your life.

Virgo with Leo

July 24–August 23

The Sun governs this dominating fixed fire sign, and the victorious Lion commands instant attention the moment it enters a room. It expects to: Leo is the great actor and director of the zodiac, and it lives its entire life as if at center stage . . . or on the jungle throne. If you should happen to be on that tawny arm at a party, don't expect to remain there for long because the entire crowd will clamor for The Presence— and beneficent Leo will have to oblige. Indeed, you may not even see your Lion again until the end of the evening when the lights go up, the music stops playing, and the guests begin to leave. Your modesty will shun, if not indeed recoil from, this feline's need to make a great splash, so you will always remain one step behind when you are out in public.

Far from bothering you, however, this situation will bring you relief: The last thing in the world you want to do is hobnob with indiscriminate masses in a desperate quest for admiration and flattery. And you will have to do almost nothing to please your Leo: Standing to the side and letting the Lion take its bows will be action enough.

But however willing you may be to take a backseat at social and public gatherings, you remain the shining star at home, which is *your* castle—and a meticulous one at that. You will have to lay down the law in the beginning (which Leo the Law-giver can respect) and let the Lion understand that in this domain it had better not shake its mane or dare to interfere. Otherwise, there will be chaos. Leo's dedication to its own creative projects can be awe-inspiring, but when it comes to paying the rent on time, this lofty king cannot be bothered. That is where your efficiency and organizational skills will save the day; and Leo, despite its loud and wild roars, will gladly, gratefully let you take those tedious tasks off its shoulders.

This pairing can lead to great ac-

complishments, with Leo as the visionary, creatively giving orders, and you as
the detail-oriented lieutenant, carrying
them out to perfection. Indeed, this
charmingly zestful egomaniac may even
inspire you to your own greatness. You
do not lack ideas, after all, but they do
need spurring; and once you get in the
mood, your mind will flow with its own
creative juices—some of which may even
impress the brilliant Lion. But you must

not make the mistake of demanding equal time. Feed your ideas slowly into that Leonine head, and sooner or later your pussycat will agree that they are superb (and then perhaps convince itself they are Leo originals). When it comes to the Lion, flattery will get you *everywhere*.

Keep doing what you do best: Analyze the situation, devise a cunning plan, and set it into motion with painstaking subtlety and zeal. Like the hunter, you will almost certainly ensnare your proud Lion; and then, like the tamer, you will take control of its magnificent heart.

Virgo with Virgo

AUGUST 24–SEPTEMBER 23

Dating another Virgo
will be like looking in the mirror. You
will see precision, fastidious care and
concern, a genuine desire to help, along
with high-wire nervousness, exalted ex-

pectations, and a genuine passion to criticize to death. Sound familiar? If you have yet to develop a firm sense of self-esteem, you had better get on the ball because your Virgin double is unlikely to cut you any slack. You may desire nothing more than someone who thinks and breathes exactly as you do, but you had better be sure because otherwise you will pay the price. Take a careful look at all those marvelous Virgin idiosyncrasies, some of which annoy even you. You could be staring them in the face for a very long time to come.

But of course it will not be entirely negative, and all of your good qualities will be repeated in your mate. If you start to list them, you could fall in love even now; and with a little luck, you may veer so close to the perfection you have always sought that your cynical and sarcastic side may never have to rear its ugly head. How wonderful it would be not to have to scold another person about eating the right foods, staying physically fit, cleaning up a mess, or have *them* bugging you about your "obsessive" concern with reason and method? Finally you have found the ideal mate. . . .

Except that you can find fault with anything and anyone, yourself (and your Virgin double) included. You criticize relentlessly—and you would certainly not hesitate to criticize another Virgo, who would also not hesitate to criticize you. Think about that for a minute: Once you have finished slamming yourself for falling short of godliness, the second Virgo would take up the chorus and add a few new verses. And if, by some miracle, you actually did something that pleased you, it would have to pass muster a second time—and probably fail. The two of you could be paragons of service and generosity, and all you could do would be to weep over your many blown chances. You and your Virgin pal could find fault with your funeral arrangements even as you are being buried.

To get this relationship off the ground, the two of you will have to find some way to cease, or at least severely diminish, your incessant faultfinding, and accentuate the many virtues you share. And since you are the intellectual and eagle-eyed analysts of the zodiac, that shouldn't be impossible. If you still insist on striving for perfection, however, then know this: That way madness lies. And double madness, therefore, will be found with another Virgo.

But if you can get beyond that pointless and impossible dream, you may be able to discover how fantastically compatible the two of you can actually be. Turn down the lights, switch off your overactive minds, and discover bliss, if not perfection. In any case, practice makes perfect! It is possible (though this may seem beyond the pale) that neither of you will ever complain again.

Virgo with Libra

SEPTEMBER 24–OCTOBER 23

*L*ibra, *symbolized by* the balancing scales of justice, is on a lifelong quest for beauty, peace, and aesthetic harmony; you eternally seek precision, serenity, and absolute perfection. In certain ways you may seem to be cut from the same bolt of cloth; and this cardinal air sign ruled by Venus, the goddess of love, could wonderfully complement all of your weaknesses and strengths. You can do the same for the Scales.

This sign, idealistic and visionary, can outline a thousand schemes of every sort; you will dot all the i's and provide practical answers to any apparently unresolvable problems that may crop up. The Scales will conjure the most passionate, dreamy-eyed images of what your life together might be; you will supply the economic projections of what is truly possible. Libra lives in the clouds, whereas you have your feet planted firmly on Earth. You can provide exactly the kind of perfect balance that Libra has always sought, and this ceaselessly elegant sign may be seductive enough to please even you.

Libra can penetrate your heart and

soul as few signs can, and you may prove powerless against that magical, romantic spell. The Scales come closer to the ideal mate than any other sign of the zodiac. They will always put you first; they will use every trick in the book to fulfill your desires, and they will make you feel as if you are floating on air. They may flatter you outrageously to make you feel good, but they will always have your best interests at heart. Libra, indeed, will place the two of you above itself, and no sign is more judicious, even-tempered, or fair-minded. With those sterling qualities staring you in the face, how could you, even in your high perfectionism, possibly turn away? All you have to do in return is provide Libra with the attention it craves—and deserves.

But too much romance, for you, is not a good thing, so you will have to inform the Scales that although you value companionship tremendously, you do not need—nor particularly desire—scented candles and champagne. You would much prefer some intellectual rigor to spice up the game. The Scales are the great diplomats of the zodiac, masters of compromise, so they surely will accommodate your demure request; and even if this indulgent and pleasure-seeking sign doesn't always enjoy your mental pursuits, it will be clever enough to convince you that it does.

In return, after Libra has listened attentively to all the details of your industrious day, you can give in with good grace to your mate's idea of a relaxing, fun-filled evening. Turn on the music, lower the lights, and put your thoughts on idle; the Scales will perform the ultimate balancing act of turning your brainstorming day into a long, loving, and passionate night. Once you surrender, Libra will light up your sensual side, which often hides in terror behind your sharp words and critical manner. After that, the Scales will never have to worry about being alone again. And you might not shun romance as much as you once did.

Virgo with
Scorpio

OCTOBER 24–NOVEMBER 22

This fixed water sign, named for the venomous desert arachnid with the legendary sting, is as tempestuous as the oceans and may well rattle the serene foundation you have worked so very hard to build. The benefits of this pairing can be enormous, but you may not be able to make the necessary changes. You are voluble in your criticism and find fault with everything and everyone, but Scorpio is the last sign you can do that with. *It does not take well to prying or complaint;* and whenever it feels menaced, whether justly or not, it responds in one of only two ways: a deadly sting or an equally deadly silence. Only the slightest provocation is required for either.

Scorpio, from long experience, trusts no one but itself. Brooding is its element, and it also takes life a notch more seriously than most other signs. It does not like to talk—does not always know how to talk, indeed—and bottles up its feelings until the pressure builds to the breaking point. And since it is also prickly even about listening, Scorpio will put up fierce resistance to any and all advice, even from a gentle, compassionate, and generous Virgin like you. If you can lay low and play your cards with judicious subtlety and put the kibosh on your very sharp tongue, you may eventually make headway. Scorpio is not idiotic: It *will* listen, if only it can figure out how, and it will in fact admire and even envy your ability to give so selflessly.

Because of its awkwardness in social

relations, Scorpio may frequently desire nothing more than that you lend a sensitive ear and act as a sounding board for its secret hopes and fears. This is where your compassion and warmth can save the day; and once the Scorpion's natural suspicions have been allayed, watch out! The zodiac contains no greater passion or coiled intensity or more fervent and heartfelt emotion. All that, harnessed by your relentlessly analytical mind, could form a new Mt. Vesuvius. The two of you need only relax and learn to trust.

Your financial triumphs can be equally grand, and the two of you will be a perfect fit in money matters. Scorpio is the shrewd master of business who wheels and deals the way a surgeon wields a scalpel; you are the careful pragmatist who understands frugality and steady fiscal planning. Just be sure to apportion your responsibilities with the greatest of care—and clarity—because neither of you can tolerate seeing anyone elbowing in on your private turf.

And when the day is done, you and somber Scorpio will need to unwind. Both of you are tense and tightly wound, but you are the more deliberate, so you should take the first step—and make sure you plan a romantic *physical* evening in which you can shut off your overburdened and endlessly complicated minds.

Once you allow the Scorpion to open up, it can open up a new sensuality in you; and after that, you will have a ferociously loyal mate you can depend on for the rest of your life.

Virgo with Sagittarius

NOVEMBER 23–DECEMBER 21

Sagittarius seeks truth
and justice in much the same way you
pursue perfection of body and mind; and
in its quest to discover the secrets of the

universe, the restless Archer, a mutable fire sign, will think nothing of journeying halfway around the world. Its symbol, after all, is the centaur shooting its idealistic arrows into the sky, and that somehow suits the most athletic, travel-oriented, and freedom-loving sign of the zodiac.

Because the Archer wants to look and feel eternally young, it shares your desire to stay in shape; and although you may differ on where you want to take your vacations, you will both agree that you are raring to go. Sagittarius is far more exotic: It will likely be torn between a culturally rich foreign capital or a hiking expedition through Tibet. You would much rather stay closer to home, but, so long as your accommodations are comfortable, you may decide to go along with the wild Sagittarian plan—especially since you fully expect the favor to be returned some day soon.

So far so good, but the Archer is the eternal optimist, whereas you worry about everything under the sun. Sagittarius is a visionary who sees the grand picture; you get fixated on trivial details. You like everything pragmatically in place; the Archer shoots for the Moon and lets the arrows fall where they may. Sagittarius leaves its belongings strewn all over the house; you will pick a single spot of lint from a chair. You save money carefully, whereas the Archer spends with frenzied abandon, and so on down the line.

Can this twosome possibly work, or will your contrasting styles only drive you apart? A good start would be to take all paychecks out of the Archer's hands, or you will have nothing before you even begin. And a little imagination wouldn't hurt, either, because Sagittarius can broaden your horizons enormously and even teach you to have fun. The Archer cherishes a great collection of books and beautiful slides of its journeys abroad, and you couldn't find a more exciting or happy-go-lucky partner. So if you insist on a mate who provides comfort and financial security, the impractical Archer might as well take its bow elsewhere; but if you are willing to take a risk, you could hit pay dirt. This Archer may not always be on target, but the detours it takes will be more fascinating than many other people's bull's-eyes.

You also have another bond, a firm belief in the golden rule: Do unto others as you would have them do unto you. You desire constantly to be of service, and the Archer would give the shirt off its back to anyone in need, so you should do everything you can to overcome your differences and make this partnership work. Truly good-hearted people do not

225

march down the street every day, and you could trust the Archer with your life. Make it your mission in life to get Sagittarius to settle down, and this challenging relationship could be the one you've been waiting for throughout your existence.

Virgo with Capricorn

DECEMBER 22–JANUARY 20

*C*apricorn, a cardinal earth sign symbolized by a goat trudging stolidly to the top of the mountain, is one of the two hardest working and most pragmatic signs of the zodiac. You are the other. Together, you come as close to perfection as any two people are likely to get, and this, miraculously, may be a match truly made in heaven.

You will expend every effort to get the job done efficiently, meticulously, and with time to spare; Capricorn will set its long-term goals into motion slowly and methodically, and will pursue them with dogged determination. You

228

like assisting and supporting; the Goat insists on taking the lead. You are speedy, whereas Capricorn is deliberate; and although you are capable of doing a variety of things at once, the Goat moves to the next undertaking only when the previous one has been completed. If Capricorn sets the goals and you bring them to fruition, you will be a highly successful and prosperous pair.

This silver lining may have a dark

cloud that leaves you with question
marks. You would rather not let petty
emotions (or indeed any emotions) veer
you off course, but you are also the
prime worrywart of the zodiac, so you
often need a shoulder to lean on and a
head to rely on. Capricorn may not be
the one. The Goat can provide all the
certainty you need to allay your financial
fears, but where emotions are concerned,
it wobbles. If you seek comforting words

and pats on the back, Capricorn will often fall short of your great expectations.

And don't unleash your biting tongue when this workaholic announces that it will be toiling late once again. Capricorn *hates* being told what to do—and the more you criticize, the longer it will stay at the office. If you say gently but firmly what you would like, your wishes will be the Goat's command. Capricorn may be ruthless in business,

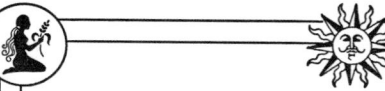

but when it comes to the person it loves, it is a pussycat—but one that detests cages.

After working its fingers to the bone from dawn till dusk, Capricorn will be thrilled to see you when it walks through the door; and because keeping a model household is one of your crowning glories, you will make home a true castle. The weary Goat will find this more gratifying still. It doesn't take much to please a doting Capricorn, but don't expect major life changes. Your mate may not give you everything you want (who could?), but it will give you everything it can, and certainly provide for all of your material needs.

And even though Capricorn may be silent until it has something to say, you will be pleasantly surprised by its body language. The world may find you all work, no play, and very dull, but the flies

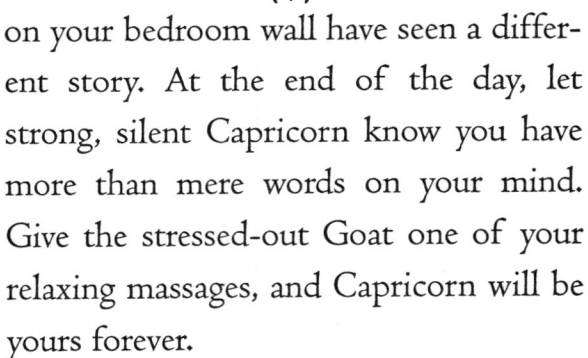

on your bedroom wall have seen a different story. At the end of the day, let strong, silent Capricorn know you have more than mere words on your mind. Give the stressed-out Goat one of your relaxing massages, and Capricorn will be yours forever.

Virgo with Aquarius

JANUARY 21–FEBRUARY 19

Fixed air sign Aquarius is symbolized by an angel pouring healing waters over the Earth, and this is one of the few signs of the zodiac that can match you for compassion and the desire to serve. Both of you are also nervous and high-strung, but you have different ways of calming yourselves. You will become obsessive about cleaning the house, filing papers, or burying yourself in work until every last *t* has been crossed. The Water Bearer will run around madly trying to reengineer the world, and the more people it meets along the way, the better.

You like to work with individuals,

but Aquarius, whose desire to save humanity exceeds even yours, is only comfortable with great masses. You operate on a case-by-case basis; Aquarius is more visionary and theoretical. Whereas you would be happy to mend a single sprained ankle, the Water Bearer wants to change the world; and although you love home and would like it to be your refuge, Aquarius sees home as a place to eat and sleep between meetings.

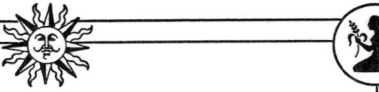

If you take up with this sign, you will have to be prepared for this casual treatment and your lack of time together. The only meal you're likely to share is the early breakfast your mate gobbles down before leaving to face the first great challenge of the day; and if you want to meet for dinner, you will have to squeeze in a quick half hour among rallies, groups, and committees. On top of all this, the Water Bearer's temperament is as volatile as your own, so if you start to complain about being neglected, a shouting match may well ensue. The Water Bearer does not like to be reminded that it is behaving badly. Aquarius chose you for a partner because it considered you its best friend, an intellectual counterpart whose emotional needs were under control, and who would therefore understand its imperative to rescue the world from itself. You do sympathize with and admire the

Water Bearer for all of its selfless concern, but still you cannot accept being last on its list of priorities.

If you can convince Aquarius that even clear-eyed intellects like yourself are filled with self-doubt from time to time, then maybe you can alert it to your own sensitivities and needs, and bring its head down out of the clouds—to some extent. In return, you may be expected to provide a listening ear and a great deal of support, which you will gladly supply. Just remind Aquarius (which you will have to keep doing) to give a little back now and again . . . and send out hints about what awaits as the evening approaches. Even the Water Bearer, though busy from morning till night, has to unwind at some point, and that is when you must force Aquarius to clear its busy schedule and mark the calendar for a romantic rendezvous. After you have tanta-

lized your partner with stimulating conversation and endless praise for its good-
hearted deeds, you can bring Aquarius
home for a nightcap it will never forget.

Virgo with Pisces

FEBRUARY 20–MARCH 20

Y*ou are quick, fastidi-*ous, and down-to-earth; Pisces is emotional, highly sentimental, and lives in a world of perpetual fantasy. At first

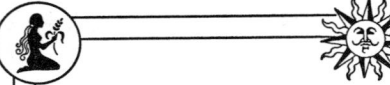

glance, this would appear to be a disaster waiting to happen. And yet it could turn out to have golden possibilities.

This mutable water sign is symbolized by two fish swimming in opposite directions, which perfectly captures the Piscean inability to make up its mind or stick to anything for very long. The Fish dreams night and day and cannot be soiled with reality; it would be perfectly happy to glide through life at its own rhythmical pace, little troubled by the rest of humanity's marching. Pisces loves people and has a rooted inability to let anything or anyone ever get it down, which is another part of its beguiling charm and childlike grace; and once it sets its bright eye upon you, you will be hooked. The question is, will you be able to accept the Fish for what it really is? If not, you had better give up now.

As the great social worker and

supreme organizer of the zodiac, you cannot wait to get your hands on Pisces and turn it into an upstanding citizen of the practical world. Yet if you did succeed in transforming the Fish into who you thought it should be, then the impressionable, good-natured, but somewhat wishy-washy soul you fell in love with would vanish from sight. All you would have left is a poor facsimile of yourself—and Pisces would probably be miserable. Unless you crave a weak mirror image, you had better start dwelling on what you both share—which is a great deal.

You are the two most compassionate, helpful, and gullible members of the zodiacal fraternity, and anyone with a problem can rely on you at any time of day or night. Although both of you adore the role of friend in need, however, there are times you wish the entire world

would leave you alone. But that would not satisfy your need to serve, and each of you will be buoyed by the other's generosity and compassion. If yours starts to fail even momentarily, the Fish will glide in with a smile of encouragement, and off you will go again. And even though you know perfectly well that the Fish's view of reality borders on the unrealistic, you may find that Piscean optimism infectious. All of a sudden, despite your pessimism, you may learn, to your own amazement, to have faith in what lies ahead.

The Fish is your polar opposite; and in the end, this relationship could provide you with the most valuable lesson of your life. Relax, and slip into the gentle Piscean stream. The Fish will entice you to shut off your relentlessly analytical brain, and then it will transport you to a world in which dreams come true, bodies move to a celestial rhythm, and you can both swim upstream for years to come. Once you let this dreamy sign take you where it wants to go, you will never talk about changing Pisces again.

You and the Moon

J*ust as the Moon takes*
a month to orbit the Earth, so it requires
approximately thirty days to pass
through, or transit, the various signs of
the zodiac—beginning with Aries, end-
ing with Pisces, and spending about two
and a half days in each. As it does so, it
exerts an extraordinary influence on our

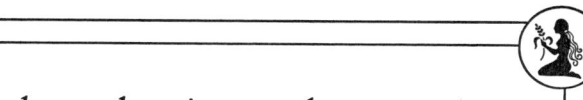

moods, much as it expends a mysterious, physical pull on the ocean's tides.

The Sun may guide our more conscious and overt qualities, but the Moon rules over our instinctive, intuitive life; when we examine our daily moon signs, we become aware of the myriad and mystical ways in which that lunar body affects our emotional weather. When it transits a fire sign, for example, we are often dominated by fiery emotions, such as

anger and passion. As it moves to an earth sign, we will feel a more rooted need for stability and comfort. The Moon in a water sign will generally bring watery emotions, like sadness and confusion; and an air-sign passage will lead to a sharpening of our thirst for knowledge.

Obviously, emotional weather isn't identical for everyone; the relationship between the position of the Moon and your particular sun sign will influence what the precise mood of the moment will be for you, and a constant subtle interplay occurs. If we pay close attention to the passages of the Moon, however, we can become far more adept at negotiating wisely and well the many challenges and changes of our daily life.

(Consult the moon charts beginning on page 332 for the time and date that the Moon enters each of the twelve signs of the zodiac throughout every month of the year from 1997 to 2005.)

The Moon in Aries

Mars, the god of war, rules Aries, a highly aggressive and provocative Moon; and although you may possess an inquisitive mind and an acid tongue, this transit will still be too much for your delicate system to bear. If you cannot find a legitimate outlet for your frustration and anger, you may unload them indiscriminately on everyone you meet—and even then you will be expected to play peacemaker on the job since you are usually the clearest-headed member of the crew. If anyone can remain cool, calm, and collected in the midst of a hurricane while pointing out the irrational behavior of others, it is

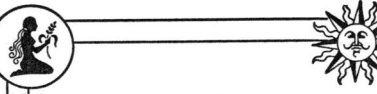

you. But be sure to mince your own words, since volatility is the key for the next few days. Anything you say cannot only be taken the wrong way, but held against you in the future.

Be similarly cautious with financial opportunities. Several interesting ones may come your way, but this Moon's impulsiveness can lead to danger. Use your common sense and plan ahead.

If you are single, your usual healthy

skepticism may suffer an overload and fail you during this busy transit when people seem to keep coming in and out of revolving doors. Take advantage and stay open to being swept off your feet, or the chance of a lifetime could pass you by. This Moon will bring its share of anger and conflict, but it will also encourage you to be assertive and direct. This is not your usual mode, but if you see someone who catches your eye, strike

up a conversation. Be daring. And by all means make yourself available for a fun-filled first date.

If you are already committed, let spontaneity rule: Do something different and exciting that you have never done before. (Mountain retreats, snorkeling holidays, or trips to Cancún.) Romantic adventures suit the Aries Moon to a *T*, and this could be the perfect time for the two of you to renew your commitment.

You should wait until the next transit, however, to bring up unresolved issues that may have been nagging at you for months. Once the Moon enters Taurus, which is governed by the goddess of love, you will be far likelier to talk rather than merely argue about your differences. And you may even discover a workable solution.

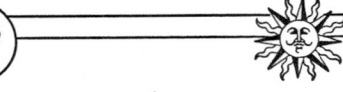

The Moon in Taurus

The Moon is exalted, or at its strongest, in Venus-ruled Taurus, and now serenity will be your reward for having made it through the impetuous and uncomfortable Aries transit. You thought then that you had been caught in a raging storm; now you have made it to a peaceful island where you can rest your head, laze around comfortably, and do the things you truly enjoy.

When lethargic, stable, and practical Taurus confronts nervous, analytical, and discriminating Virgo, your pragmatism will grow even stronger; but although you are high-strung by nature, this extremely slow-footed influence will also

steady your nerves and keep you on an even keel. You may even dream of traveling abroad or going back to school to polish old skills or learn new ones, and any practical information you acquire over the next few days can make a difference in your life for years to come. Your financial acumen is likely to be especially sharp under the influence of this monetary transit, so don't be surprised if a magnificent offer comes your way. Seize

it, by all means. You and Taurus are sensible earth signs, so you will continue to be frugal, judicious, and wise during this passage. Any decisions you make will almost certainly be the right ones.

If you are single and anxious to begin a new relationship, you have just hit the jackpot. The Taurus Moon provides exactly the right blend of sensual enjoyment and practical considerations to help you distinguish between infatuation and

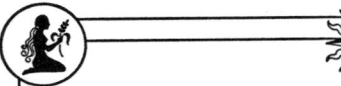

love, so you can trust your instincts and keep your healthy skepticism under wraps. If you allow pessimism to obscure your judgment, the gentle, steady, and affectionate partner you crave could easily pass in the night.

If you are already involved, this is the perfect time for you and your partner to review your financial situation and then make plans for a long overdue vacation. Take full advantage of the open lines of communication and calm, passionate mood that will blanket you under the exalted Taurus Moon. Give in to its spell. You will be surprisingly satisfied spending quiet, romantic evenings at home listening to music, dining by candlelight, or falling asleep in your lover's arms. And be sure to savor the silence, because the talkative and restless Gemini Moon now looms.

The Moon in Gemini

During the passage through loquacious Gemini, family and friends may surround you as they have never done before. Even former acquaintances you haven't seen in years could pop up unexpectedly, along with new ones with whom you may turn out to have a great deal in common. You and Gemini are both ruled by Mercury, so movement and variety will be the order of the day. Indeed, you may have so much going on that you will have to prepare the guest room to accommodate out-of-town visitors—and then apologize for not being able to spend sufficient time with them.

If you have been trying to expand your professional contacts, you will see the payoff now. Indeed, you could be so inundated by offers that you will have to call into play all of your discrimination and analytical prowess in order to negotiate them to best advantage.

This is also a propitious Moon if you are searching for someone to share your life. Normally you have difficulty introducing yourself or even making small talk, which generally strikes you as undignified and forced. Not now. You will be eager to cut to the chase in order to discover what you have or do not have in common. Then you will want to take full advantage of that knowledge—and enjoy yourself along the way. And you must do it now, because in another few days the Moon will enter domestic Cancer, and you will have a much harder time getting out of the house.

If you are already attached, you should use this highly communicative and rational influence to see that you and your partner discuss all of the unfinished business that you have been meaning to take care of over the last several weeks. You will feel particularly insightful and clearheaded about what you want to say, but make sure that you also listen attentively to the other side. After you have vanquished your little misunderstandings, you can then change your scenery and get out of the house, the last time you may do so for a while. See a movie, go to a concert, do anything that both of you enjoy. Thus stimulated, you will appreciate all the more the delights to be explored at the end of a fulfilling day.

The Moon in Cancer

*T*he Moon rules Can-
cer, which is one the most pessimistic
and worrisome signs of the zodiac, so all
of your worst tendencies will be accentuated during this transit. Your natural bent

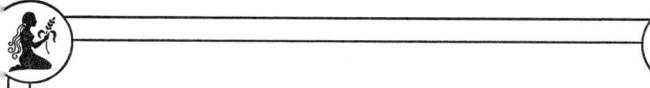

for fretting about the future and living in a state of perpetual anxiety could become a cross that even *you* cannot bear, and all you may really want to do is vanish (as the Crab retreats into its shell) and shun everyone around you.

This, however, is precisely what you should not do because Cancer is the most maternal of all zodiacal signs, and this Moon will supply loving comfort from family, friends, and colleagues.

Socializing with those who care about you could instantly clarify all of your confusion and help you to put your life into perspective. You may even begin to realize how much of your incessant worrying stems from an overactive mind playing too many tricks on you.

If you would like to change your single status, take heart: Anyone you meet during this sensitive, warm, and protective passage will probably be seeking the same kind of permanence that has eluded you for so long. All you need is a little romance. Instead of choosing an expensive but noisy restaurant in which neither of you can hear what the other is saying, go to an elegant and subdued nook that will allow you to procure each other's undivided attention. Then select a dimly lit table in a secluded corner and start gazing into those expressive eyes. Or take another tack entirely and

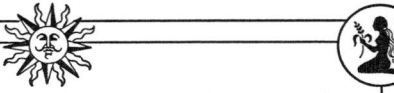

whip up a splendid home-cooked meal. Only a stone could resist the promise of familial unity and domestic bliss under this comforting and ultradreamy Moon.

If you are already involved, make your next evening at home an unforgettable one. Review and discuss your finances—and then take a break from serious endeavors and enjoy the love nest you have spent so much time decorating and putting into perfect order . . . especially, perhaps, the bedroom. You will not be in a money-spending mood, so you will have all the more incentive to entertain yourselves in highly romantic fashion. Turn the lights down low, share a delicious dessert, cuddle up with a sentimental video, and then make beautiful music together. This could remind you of the symphonies you composed when you first met.

The Moon in Leo

It *might seem as if* everyone wants a slice of you under the magnanimous, dramatic, but self-serving Leo Moon, and people will try to exploit your innate generosity. The Lion, however, which is ruled by the Sun, expects to be the center of its own solar system; and during this magnetic transit, you will suddenly feel that *your* problems should take precedence over everything else— and rightly so. Jump in with gusto and put yourself at the head of the line. You do not have to turn your back on others, but you can—at least for the next few days—resolve your own predicaments first. Whatever is left over will, as always,

be given to the rest of the world. But this strong yet generous Moon will finally provide you with the strength to take a definite stand on how you prefer to dole out your valuable time.

Leo is highly conducive to romance, and during this transit you may very possibly meet some incredibly charismatic and generous charmer who, like yourself, is ready to commit and settle down. Extroverts will be the rule rather than the exception, so you will either submit entirely to their dominance or borrow a little of their spirit. Shoot for the latter; this will be the time to showcase your best qualities, and prospective lovers could be dazzled by your analytical mind and radiant wit. But be sure to relax and open up a little more than usual on your first date, or your cool, aloof demeanor could undo all of your best intentions. It would be a pity to waste this Moon.

If you are already attached, you may be showered with delightfully unexpected presents and the kind of treatment usually reserved for royalty. This ostentatious and magnanimous Moon will bring out all of your and your partner's deepest generosity, and you may suddenly feel as if you are on your second honeymoon. Maybe you will be. You never say "I love you" often enough. Say it now—and then show it. Have a ball and leap into all those sensual pleasures you usually deny yourself when life gets you down. The Virgo Moon is next, and that will bring out all of your needless, but familiar, anxiety about the future. Until then, you can have some fun.

The Moon in Virgo

Restless, verbose, and nervous. When the Moon transits your own sign, you will need every relaxation technique in the book just to survive. All of your anxieties will be accentuated and redoubled, so you may want to throw yourself into physical exercise, even to the point of exhaustion, in order to burn off tension and clear your mind. Swim, run, dance; do anything you have to or can. And do it quickly, because yours is the Moon of pragmatism, and numerous projects will loom on the horizon. Any one of them could further your career and improve your financial opportunities, but until you conquer your need to worry

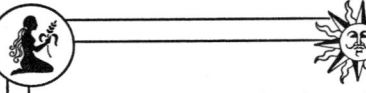

constantly (which will be twice as driving now), you will be in no position to take advantage. The chance of a lifetime could pass you by.

If you are single and seeking the person of your dreams, this Moon may prove very tricky. The Virgo transit could make you even more analytical, critical, and self-conscious than you already are, and heighten all of your tensions. It could also accentuate your tenderness and sensitivity, and make you melt at life's myriad possibilities. In the first case, you should do everything you can to get yourself into tip-top shape and boost your self-esteem. In the second, you may become a little too vulnerable to sweet talk and false promises. You will have a fine line to tread between being ready for romance and being desperate for love, but if you keep your senses about you, you won't have to worry about

taking a miserable fall. In any case, don't despair: When the Moon enters romantic and affectionate Libra, which always has marriage on its mind, you will be in the proper position to respond to another's charms.

If you are already committed, you may find it difficult to overcome your own anxieties long enough to be sensitive to your partner's needs. Try. It is critical to open up and confide all of your hopes and fears, or your mate will be powerless to help you. Once you unload this weighty burden, a marvelous relief will sweep through you, and your partner's response could provide surprising thrills. Then you can relish—to the hilt—all of the intellectual and creative stimulation that the Virgo Moon supplies.

The Moon in Libra

Modest, *hardwork-*ing, and sensual Virgo meets elegant, judicious, and highly romantic Libra. Nervous Mercury meets Venus, and the creative juices will flow as they have never done before. Self-improvement will flower, and if you have ever toyed with taking a new course, changing your instructors, polishing your talents and skills, or otherwise consolidating your many considerable abilities, do so now with full confidence. Libra will supply the aesthetic discrimination; you will provide the discipline and hard work, and you may reach a new professional level that could shoot you into the financial

stars. This is an ideal time to spread your ideas and vision liberally; and since Libra is the king of connection and the ultimate networker of the zodiac, you might also find the perfect partner to inject the right kind of vitality into your life—both personally and professionally.

If you are single and in the market for a new relationship, this is the best of all possible Moons for you. Romance is in the stars, the flowers, the air. Drink deeply, and then drink again. This is exactly the transit you need to break out of your self-consciousness (or self-absorption) and *concentrate* on the person across the dinner table. If you take the time to discover common interests, you may ignite that special spark—which could ignite a brushfire. But this lovely transit could cause you to see potential sparks everywhere, so be careful not to swoon at everyone you meet. Use your common sense and sharp powers of

discrimination, and you should be fine.

If you are already committed, the amorous Libra Moon will bring back the heady days of first love and blushing romance, and you should renew your vows by spending time alone. Dash away for the weekend, far from the madding crowd. Even *very* far from the madding crowd: Your finances should be healthy at the moment, so don't be afraid to splurge by planning an exotic vacation to another continent or hemisphere. But whatever you choose to do over the next few days, try not to bring up any bones of contention: You wouldn't want to interfere with the sublime harmony that this wonderful Moon unselfishly provides. Once you enter provocative Scorpio, peace and quiet may be a thing of the past.

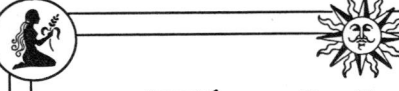

The Moon in Scorpio

The Moon is fallen, or weakened, in Scorpio, an intensely provocative and brooding transit, and *everyone* will seem sullen and overserious during the next few days. You may intensely scrutinize every move you make; your obsessiveness may drive not only you but all of your friends to distraction, but at all costs you should try to look at the lighter side. Cling to your sense of humor even if it appears that the entire world has gone haywire, and you could come out on top. For when you combine your own meticulousness and pragmatism with Scorpio's obstinacy and ferocious determination, you may finally have

the combustible mixture that will allow you to take charge of your personal and professional life. The Scorpion, when threatened, digs into the sand and flashes its pincers and stinging tail. You, in an infinitely more moderated and decorous way, can do the same.

This very serious transit will add further introspection to your already reserved personality, so if you are single and looking for someone to share your life, you could end up even more self-conscious than usual and therefore more awkward at trying to make an impression. On the other hand, the Scorpio Moon is one of the most fervent and passionate in existence, so any emotions or physical desires that *are* aroused over the next few days will probably dig deep and remain entrenched. A Scorpion will never give up. If you meet someone who makes you feel special, don't squander the

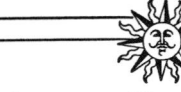

opportunity even if you are fidgety, worried, or uncomfortable. Once the sociable Sagittarius Moon comes calling, your uncertainty will seem a thing of the past.

If you are already committed, you will undergo a tempestuous series of emotional highs and lows. This Moon will magnify every problem you possess, so you should bring to the fore all of your minor irritations and complaints: They could grow into monstrous proportions if they are not nipped in the bud quickly. Once you have cleared the air and your mind, you should tell your partner how special you feel whenever you're together. Then you can surrender to the passion you both feel whenever you look into each other's eyes. The Scorpio Moon will take care of the rest and provide some of the most exciting and adventurous days you will ever remember.

The Moon in Sagittarius

Now *that the prickly* Scorpio transit is over, you can start to embrace the Moon's passage through social and idealistic Sagittarius. Brooding will be replaced by enthusiasm, pessimism by optimism, and you will have the rare and unfathomable feeling that you can conquer the world. Blind faith may conflict with your usual tendency to worry needlessly and analyze everything to death, but this happy-go-lucky influence might induce you to try something new without knowing what the outcome will be. Taking a spontaneous trip, buying a new wardrobe, or even planning a bold business venture may well occupy you over

the next few days. And because the pursuit of knowledge is a favorite Sagittarian pastime, don't be surprised if you sign up for a course, spend more time in the library, or take a joyride along the information superhighway. Just be certain you don't completely blow your paycheck searching for the exotic. Interesting activities depend more on the imagination than on moola.

Under the influence of this extroverted and athletic Moon, you may run into a stranger on one of your customary outdoor jaunts who, like yourself, is looking for someone special. You will be brimming with self-esteem, so you should have no difficulty taking the lead and making the initial introduction. Even if romantic sparks do not immediately fly, the two of you will be enthralled by fascinating conversation. And no matter what else happens, you will have made a friend you can rely on for years to come.

If you are already involved, this would be an excellent time for you and your partner to ignore your busy schedules and dedicate the next few days to having fun. Sagittarius is the great traveler of the zodiac, so you should avoid your secure and comfortable surroundings and explore new terrain. Driving through the countryside, winding around narrow mountain roads, or hiking along some mountain trails will satisfy your craving for healthy activity; and savoring an expensive, three-course meal in an atmospheric restaurant, topped by a sensual night in a remote country inn will fulfill your desire for indulgence without being *too* excessive. Why resist the blandishments of this fun-loving Moon? Take advantage now because once you enter serious Capricorn, you will start counting your pennies. But what a wonderful couple of days it will have been with the Sagittarius Moon!

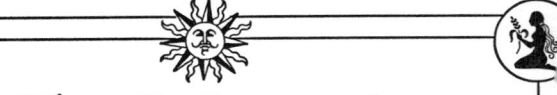

The Moon in Capricorn

The Moon is detrimen-
tal, or not very comfortable, in Saturn-
ruled Capricorn, so the more judicious
and cautious aspects of your personality
will rise to the top again. You were jovial

and full of energy during the last transit, but now you will be staid, melancholy, and desirous of staying put. You will probably find yourself reading a sentimental book or watching an old sappy movie. This is the time to straighten out any misunderstandings that may have arisen recently at home or at work, and professional goals will also be high on your list of priorities. Although you are not at all in the mood for socializing, you

do have lots of energy when it comes to your job.

Indeed, you will now be in a position to initiate your ambitious plans, so you should do everything you can to rally the support of your colleagues. They will be especially attentive to your practical ideas, which can bring financial rewards to everyone concerned. You may also be inundated by requests for the sound and practical advice at which you have always excelled, though you would probably offer it whether solicited or not. But do try to be more diplomatic and less moralistic when you are called upon for unconditional support. Don't make other people feel bad just because you're in a bit of a sour mood.

If you are single and trying to connect with someone special, this is the time for frivolity to end and seriousness to begin. Attending media events and so-

cializing with large groups of people will be less beneficial to you than a little heart-to-heart conversation. And although you are usually ill at ease when you meet someone new, you will now have an overwhelming urge to cut the preliminaries and find out quickly if the two of you are compatible. That could be motivation enough to get beyond your shyness. Others you meet are also likely to feel the sting of self-consciousness, so your efforts should pay off.

If you are already committed, many of your activities will revolve around getting your bills paid, planning for the future, and spending time with your family and friends. You may feel lethargic and will not have an overwhelming desire to venture far from home. Why not invite a few friends over for dinner so you can show off your culinary skills as well as your comfortable digs? Or better yet, en-

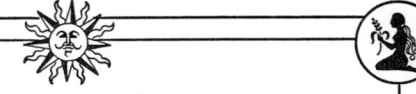

joy a little tête-à-tête with your partner. Now is the time to give each other the languorous attention you deserve, because once the Moon enters restless and quixotic Aquarius, you will be far too busy.

The Moon in Aquarius

This will be an unset-tling, yet exciting, period you are unlikely to forget. Your work schedule will be so overloaded with deadlines, appointments, and last-minute scheduling changes that you will barely have time to sit down and eat a decent meal, let alone keep up with your usual exercise regime. Indeed, it would require a virtual miracle (or a master juggler) to balance all the social engagements, professional responsibilities, and volunteer work you have on your plate. If anyone can do it, however, it is you. You *enjoy* keeping busy, and since everyone you know will be whirling like a dervish, you will be in perfect company.

But be sure that your juggling does indeed leave room for personal commitments. Those you love may be very understanding, but they also need—and deserve—a little attention in return.

If you are single and eager to find someone interested in a permanent commitment, be patient. These frenetic times will make it easy to *meet* people, but they may also make it impossible to pencil in a first date. You may not have the time;

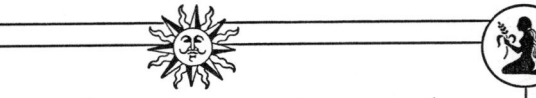

you may not have the space in your calendar. But try to squeeze in a cup of coffee if nothing else because even those few precious minutes could be all you need to click—and to do anything you can to synchronize your schedules. And given your own workaholic nature, someone whose daily routine is as cluttered as your own could be exactly what you are looking for. (Among other things, you would never again have to apologize for letting your professional duties take precedence over your personal life.)

Even if you are permanently involved, scheduling problems will be no less bewildering or hectic. This is the ultimate Moon of social engagement, so simply accept the fact that the two of you will only collide early in the morning or late at night—and fire up the microwave a little more often than usual. And because both of you will be over-

worked, exhausted, but fulfilled at the end of the day, whatever moments you *can* squeeze in together should be special ones filled with love and affection. The Aquarius whirlwind will soon wear off, and then you will soar into the Pisces Moon—the most sensitive, impressionable, and romantic transit of all.

The Moon in Pisces

Pisces leads the zodiac in emotion, compassion, and indulgence. It is also your polar opposite, so this entrancing passage will diffuse an unmistakable aura of creativity and artistic

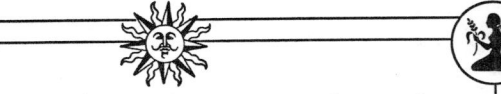

sensibility, and you can now take a de-
served rest from the frenzy of the last
few days.

But Pisces is also the most aimless
sign in existence, and this transit will not
always sit well with your hardworking
persona. Yet there is no point in fighting:
You had better give in to the lethargy
that pours over you for the next few days,
or you will spend an enormous amount
of energy uselessly. Take in a concert; go

to a movie; file through an exhibit at a gallery or museum. You *need* to take a break now; it will stimulate your mind and pleasantly fill in the gaps when you aren't working.

Under the influence of this highly sentimental but unrealistic Moon, you may fall in love with anyone who so much as bats an eyelash at you. You often have difficulty meeting people who arouse even the slightest interest, but

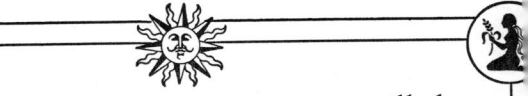

during the Pisces transit you will be flooded by interested parties. Many of them would simply like to have fun with no promise of future obligations, but your keen eye and keener analytical abilities will easily slash through the dashing, attractive surfaces and cut to the truth of what lies beneath. Once you have done that and have found the one you seek, you will be carried away by a sublime wave of unabashed romanticism and hope for a glorious future. That is the Pisces way.

If you are already attached, the two of you will finally be bathed in a serene and sensual light that will allow you to stop talking and start staring raptly into each other's eyes. You will gush with so much passion, indeed, that others will eagerly leave you alone. Friends and family will be happy to see that you have taken time out of your busy schedules to recap-

ture the magic that brought you together in the first place. When it starts to glow, lock all the doors, turn off the phone, and sail away on an ocean of dreams. Take full advantage of this escapist mood now because the Moon will soon transit aggressive Aries again, and the entire cycle will begin anew.

Moon

Charts

1997–2005

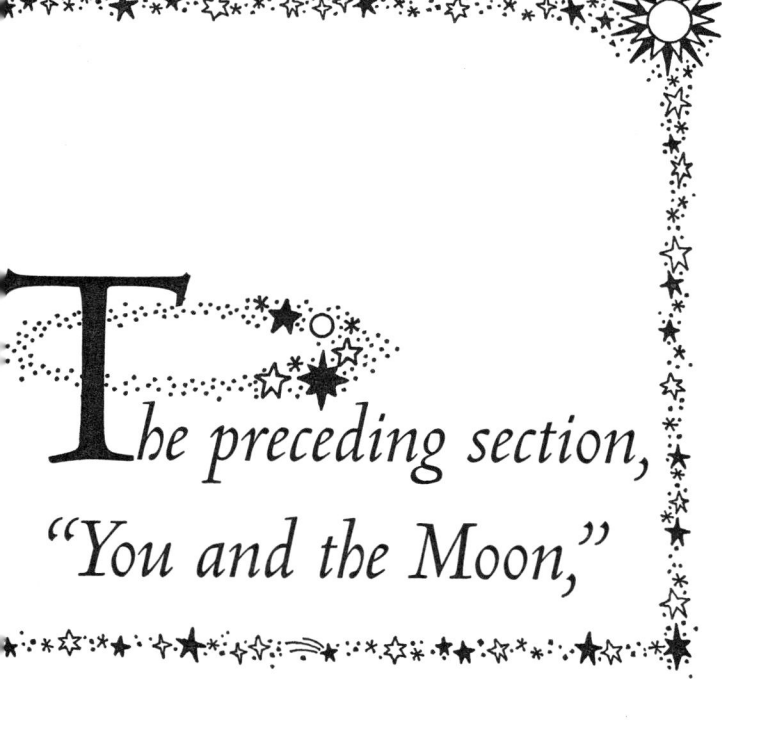

The preceding section, "You and the Moon,"

explained in detail how the Moon affects your emotions and behavior as it moves through the twelve signs of the zodiac. It takes approximately thirty days for the Moon to pass through, or transit, the twelve signs—spending about two and a half days in each. So every month, for the short period that the Moon is moving through Leo, or Aries, or Scorpio (or any other sign), you can take advantage of the Moon's positive or negative influences.

The following charts show the date and time the Moon enters each sign of the zodiac. Just look up the current date (charts are provided for the years 1997 through 2005); the sign that precedes the date indicates the Moon's current transit. For instance, in the two following transits

Can Jan 10 19:43

Leo Jan 13 02:45

the Moon enters the sign of Cancer on

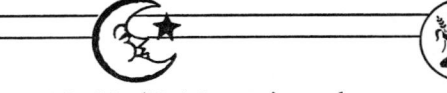

January 10 at 19:43 (7:43 P.M.) and stays in that sign until entering the sign of Leo on January 13 at 02:45 (2:45 A.M.). All times are eastern standard time in a twenty-four-hour clock format: 00:01–12:00 (noon) are the A.M. hours; 12:01–24:00 (midnight) are the P.M. hours (from 13:00 to 24:00, subtract 12 to translate into P.M.).

1997

Sco Jan 03 08:00	Sag Feb 01 23:49	Aqu Mar 05 14:53
Sag Jan 05 14:26	Cap Feb 04 03:43	Pis Mar 07 14:56
Cap Jan 07 16:54	Aqu Feb 06 04:20	Ari Mar 09 14:32
Aqu Jan 09 16:59	Pis Feb 08 03:33	Tau Mar 11 15:38
Pis Jan 11 16:50	Ari Feb 10 03:29	Gem Mar 13 19:49
Ari Jan 13 18:21	Tau Feb 12 05:56	Can Mar 16 03:51
Tau Jan 15 22:40	Gem Feb 14 11:54	Leo Mar 18 15:08
Gem Jan 18 05:53	Can Feb 16 21:12	Vir Mar 21 03:59
Can Jan 20 15:28	Leo Feb 19 08:52	Lib Mar 23 16:34
Leo Jan 23 02:50	Vir Feb 21 21:38	Sco Mar 26 03:41
Vir Jan 25 15:26	Lib Feb 24 10:22	Sag Mar 28 12:38
Lib Jan 28 04:21	Sco Feb 26 21:55	Cap Mar 30 19:06
Sco Jan 30 15:47	Sag Mar 01 07:00	Aqu Apr 01 22:57
	Cap Mar 03 12:37	Pis Apr 04 00:41

Ari Apr 06 01:19	Gem May 07 15:21	Leo Jun 08 14:58
Tau Apr 08 02:21	Can May 09 21:13	Vir Jun 11 02:43
Gem Apr 10 05:27	Leo May 12 06:32	Lib Jun 13 15:35
Can Apr 12 12:04	Vir May 14 18:43	Sco Jun 16 02:50
Leo Apr 14 22:22	Lib May 17 07:26	Sag Jun 18 10:37
Vir Apr 17 11:00	Sco May 19 18:11	Cap Jun 20 15:01
Lib Apr 19 23:35	Sag May 22 01:49	Aqu Jun 22 17:20
Sco Apr 22 10:17	Cap May 24 06:50	Pis Jun 24 19:08
Sag Apr 24 18:31	Aqu May 26 10:19	Ari Jun 26 21:38
Cap Apr 27 00:31	Pis May 28 13:17	Tau Jun 29 01:23
Aqu Apr 29 04:49	Ari May 30 16:17	Gem Jul 01 06:35
Pis May 01 07:49	Tau Jun 01 19:39	Can Jul 03 13:33
Ari May 03 09:59	Gem Jun 03 23:55	Leo Jul 05 22:45
Tau May 05 12:04	Can Jun 06 06:01	Vir Jul 08 10:22

Lib Jul 10 23:20	Sag Aug 12 04:44	Aqu Sep 12 23:08
Sco Jul 13 11:19	Cap Aug 14 10:40	Pis Sep 14 23:58
Sag Jul 15 20:01	Aqu Aug 16 12:57	Ari Sep 16 23:25
Cap Jul 18 00:44	Pis Aug 18 13:00	Tau Sep 18 23:22
Aqu Jul 20 02:28	Ari Aug 20 12:45	Gem Sep 21 01:39
Pis Jul 22 02:59	Tau Aug 22 13:58	Can Sep 23 07:33
Ari Jul 24 04:03	Gem Aug 24 17:56	Leo Sep 25 17:12
Tau Jul 26 06:53	Can Aug 27 01:11	Vir Sep 28 05:27
Gem Jul 28 12:04	Leo Aug 29 11:19	Lib Sep 30 18:32
Can Jul 30 19:38	Vir Aug 31 23:27	Sco Oct 03 06:57
Leo Aug 02 05:26	Lib Sep 03 12:29	Sag Oct 05 17:42
Vir Aug 04 17:15	Sco Sep 06 01:08	Cap Oct 08 02:02
Lib Aug 07 06:16	Sag Sep 08 11:53	Aqu Oct 10 07:28
Sco Aug 09 18:49	Cap Sep 10 19:22	Pis Oct 12 09:58

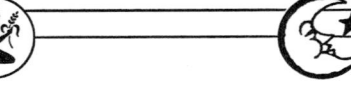

Ari Oct 14 10:24	Gem Nov 14 22:05	Leo Dec 16 17:57
Tau Oct 16 10:16	Can Nov 17 01:33	Vir Dec 19 03:59
Gem Oct 18 11:27	Leo Nov 19 08:38	Lib Dec 21 16:34
Can Oct 20 15:45	Vir Nov 21 19:32	Sco Dec 24 05:06
Leo Oct 23 00:10	Lib Nov 24 08:29	Sag Dec 26 15:06
Vir Oct 25 11:59	Sco Nov 26 20:42	Cap Dec 28 21:47
Lib Oct 28 01:04	Sag Nov 29 06:28	Aqu Dec 31 01:57
Sco Oct 30 13:14	Cap Dec 01 13:37	
Sag Nov 01 23:25	Aqu Dec 03 18:57	**1998**
Cap Nov 04 07:30	Pis Dec 05 23:06	Pis Jan 02 04:55
Aqu Nov 06 13:32	Ari Dec 08 02:23	Ari Jan 04 07:43
Pis Nov 08 17:34	Tau Dec 10 04:59	Tau Jan 06 10:52
Ari Nov 10 19:43	Gem Dec 12 07:35	Gem Jan 08 14:42
Tau Nov 12 20:45	Can Dec 14 11:25	Can Jan 10 19:43

Leo Jan 13 02:45	Lib Feb 14 08:17	Sag Mar 18 15:55
Vir Jan 15 12:31	Sco Feb 16 21:12	Cap Mar 21 01:41
Lib Jan 18 00:44	Sag Feb 19 08:55	Aqu Mar 23 08:00
Sco Jan 20 13:33	Cap Feb 21 17:29	Pis Mar 25 10:41
Sag Jan 23 00:23	Aqu Feb 23 22:08	Ari Mar 27 10:48
Cap Jan 25 07:38	Pis Feb 25 23:41	Tau Mar 29 10:06
Aqu Jan 27 11:25	Ari Feb 27 23:42	Gem Mar 31 10:38
Pis Jan 29 13:07	Tau Mar 02 00:01	Can Apr 02 14:10
Ari Jan 31 14:21	Gem Mar 04 02:15	Leo Apr 04 21:36
Tau Feb 02 16:24	Can Mar 06 07:26	Vir Apr 07 08:25
Gem Feb 04 20:09	Leo Mar 08 15:45	Lib Apr 09 21:04
Can Feb 07 01:57	Vir Mar 11 02:35	Sco Apr 12 09:55
Leo Feb 09 09:57	Lib Mar 13 14:57	Sag Apr 14 21:51
Vir Feb 11 20:09	Sco Mar 16 03:50	Cap Apr 17 08:04

Aqu Apr 19 15:40	Ari May 21 06:05	Gem Jun 21 16:26
Pis Apr 21 20:04	Tau May 23 07:05	Can Jun 23 18:38
Ari Apr 23 21:29	Gem May 25 07:25	Leo Jun 25 23:04
Tau Apr 25 21:08	Can May 27 08:59	Vir Jun 28 06:54
Gem Apr 27 20:55	Leo May 29 13:39	Lib Jun 30 18:04
Can Apr 29 22:58	Vir May 31 22:21	Sco Jul 03 06:45
Leo May 02 04:49	Lib Jun 03 10:16	Sag Jul 05 18:23
Vir May 04 14:47	Sco Jun 05 23:04	Cap Jul 08 03:26
Lib May 07 03:18	Sag Jun 08 10:33	Aqu Jul 10 09:51
Sco May 09 16:09	Cap Jun 10 19:49	Pis Jul 12 14:21
Sag May 12 03:47	Aqu Jun 13 03:02	Ari Jul 14 17:44
Cap May 14 13:37	Pis Jun 15 08:30	Tau Jul 16 20:33
Aqu May 16 21:29	Ari Jun 17 12:22	Gem Jul 18 23:18
Pis May 19 03:02	Tau Jun 19 14:47	Can Jul 21 02:43

Leo Jul 23 07:48	Lib Aug 24 10:02	Sag Sep 25 18:04
Vir Jul 25 15:34	Sco Aug 26 22:25	Cap Sep 28 05:29
Lib Jul 28 02:14	Sag Aug 29 10:54	Aqu Sep 30 13:51
Sco Jul 30 14:44	Cap Aug 31 21:21	Pis Oct 02 18:22
Sag Aug 02 02:47	Aqu Sep 03 04:19	Ari Oct 04 19:31
Cap Aug 04 12:16	Pis Sep 05 07:46	Tau Oct 06 18:57
Aqu Aug 06 18:30	Ari Sep 07 08:52	Gem Oct 08 18:43
Pis Aug 08 22:03	Tau Sep 09 09:16	Can Oct 10 20:49
Ari Aug 11 00:09	Gem Sep 11 10:40	Leo Oct 13 02:25
Tau Aug 13 02:04	Can Sep 13 14:20	Vir Oct 15 11:32
Gem Aug 15 04:45	Leo Sep 15 20:48	Lib Oct 17 23:02
Can Aug 17 08:55	Vir Sep 18 05:51	Sco Oct 20 11:36
Leo Aug 19 15:00	Lib Sep 20 16:57	Sag Oct 23 00:15
Vir Aug 21 23:21	Sco Sep 23 05:21	Cap Oct 25 12:03

Aqu Oct 27 21:42	Ari Nov 28 15:32	Gem Dec 30 02:21
Pis Oct 30 03:57	Tau Nov 30 16:51	
Ari Nov 01 06:26	Gem Dec 02 16:29	**1999**
Tau Nov 03 06:11	Can Dec 04 16:27	Can Jan 01 03:15
Gem Nov 05 05:10	Leo Dec 06 18:55	Leo Jan 03 05:30
Can Nov 07 05:39	Vir Dec 09 01:22	Vir Jan 05 10:50
Leo Nov 09 09:33	Lib Dec 11 11:43	Lib Jan 07 19:52
Vir Nov 11 17:36	Sco Dec 14 00:16	Sco Jan 10 07:48
Lib Nov 14 04:57	Sag Dec 16 12:46	Sag Jan 12 20:22
Sco Nov 16 17:40	Cap Dec 18 23:54	Cap Jan 15 07:27
Sag Nov 19 06:12	Aqu Dec 21 09:15	Aqu Jan 17 16:10
Cap Nov 21 17:44	Pis Dec 23 16:44	Pis Jan 19 22:39
Aqu Nov 24 03:42	Ari Dec 25 22:02	Ari Jan 22 03:24
Pis Nov 26 11:12	Tau Dec 28 01:03	Tau Jan 24 06:51

Gem Jan 26 09:28	Leo Feb 26 22:44	Lib Mar 30 20:49
Can Jan 28 11:56	Vir Mar 01 05:04	Sco Apr 02 07:48
Leo Jan 30 15:16	Lib Mar 03 13:34	Sag Apr 04 20:07
Vir Feb 01 20:37	Sco Mar 06 00:22	Cap Apr 07 08:38
Lib Feb 04 04:55	Sag Mar 08 12:45	Aqu Apr 09 19:23
Sco Feb 06 16:06	Cap Mar 11 00:52	Pis Apr 12 02:33
Sag Feb 09 04:37	Aqu Mar 13 10:30	Ari Apr 14 05:45
Cap Feb 11 16:09	Pis Mar 15 16:29	Tau Apr 16 06:06
Aqu Feb 14 00:55	Ari Mar 17 19:12	Gem Apr 18 05:38
Pis Feb 16 06:39	Tau Mar 19 20:08	Can Apr 20 06:27
Ari Feb 18 10:05	Gem Mar 21 21:05	Leo Apr 22 10:06
Tau Feb 20 12:28	Can Mar 23 23:34	Vir Apr 24 17:03
Gem Feb 22 14:53	Leo Mar 26 04:22	Lib Apr 27 02:46
Can Feb 24 18:08	Vir Mar 28 11:34	Sco Apr 29 14:12

Sag May 02 02:35   Aqu Jun 03 08:35   Tau Jul 07 10:20
Cap May 04 15:11   Ari Jun 08 00:06   Gem Jul 09 11:58
Aqu May 07 02:39   Tau Jun 10 02:42   Can Jul 11 12:27
Pis May 09 11:14   Gem Jun 12 02:47   Leo Jul 13 13:26
Ari May 11 15:51   Can Jun 14 02:14   Vir Jul 15 16:38
Tau May 13 16:55   Leo Jun 16 03:07   Lib Jul 17 23:20
Gem May 15 16:07   Vir Jun 18 07:12   Sco Jul 20 09:30
Can May 17 15:39   Lib Jun 20 15:10   Sag Jul 22 21:47
Leo May 19 17:36   Sco Jun 23 02:17   Cap Jul 25 10:07
Vir May 21 23:16   Sag Jun 25 14:50   Aqu Jul 27 20:53
Lib May 24 08:29   Cap Jun 28 03:10   Pis Jul 30 05:26
Sco May 26 20:04   Aqu Jun 30 14:18   Ari Aug 01 11:45
Sag May 29 08:36   Pis Jul 02 23:33   Tau Aug 05 18:56
Cap May 31 21:04   Ari Jul 05 06:20   Can Aug 07 20:52

346

Leo Aug 09 22:55	Lib Sep 10 17:15	Sag Oct 12 21:18
Vir Aug 12 02:21	Sco Sep 13 02:08	Cap Oct 15 10:02
Lib Aug 14 08:24	Sag Sep 15 13:34	Aqu Oct 17 22:15
Sco Aug 16 17:39	Cap Sep 18 02:12	Pis Oct 20 07:31
Sag Aug 19 05:31	Aqu Sep 20 13:36	Ari Oct 22 12:39
Cap Aug 21 17:59	Pis Sep 22 21:49	Tau Oct 24 14:24
Aqu Aug 24 04:48	Ari Sep 25 02:32	Gem Oct 26 14:33
Pis Aug 26 12:48	Tau Sep 27 04:49	Can Oct 28 15:09
Ari Aug 28 18:08	Gem Sep 29 06:20	Leo Oct 30 17:46
Tau Aug 30 21:39	Can Oct 01 08:31	Vir Nov 01 23:07
Gem Sep 02 00:24	Leo Oct 03 12:13	Lib Nov 04 06:56
Can Sep 04 03:09	Vir Oct 05 17:39	Sco Nov 06 16:45
Leo Sep 06 06:28	Lib Oct 08 00:51	Sag Nov 09 04:14
Vir Sep 08 10:56	Sco Oct 10 10:01	Cap Nov 11 16:59

Aqu Nov 14 05:44	Ari Dec 16 07:28	Ari Jan 12 13:46
Pis Nov 16 16:19	Tau Dec 18 11:43	Tau Jan 14 19:36
Ari Nov 18 22:55	Gem Dec 20 12:37	Gem Jan 16 22:23
Tau Nov 21 01:24	Can Dec 22 11:52	Can Jan 18 23:00
Gem Nov 23 01:13	Leo Dec 24 11:32	Leo Jan 20 22:58
Can Nov 25 00:29	Vir Dec 26 13:34	Vir Jan 23 00:07
Leo Nov 27 01:19	Lib Dec 28 19:14	Lib Jan 25 04:09
Vir Nov 29 05:10	Sco Dec 31 04:36	Sco Jan 27 12:01
Lib Dec 01 12:29		Sag Jan 29 23:17
Sco Dec 03 22:35	**2000**	Cap Feb 01 12:09
Sag Dec 06 10:27	Sag Jan 02 16:31	Aqu Feb 04 00:30
Cap Dec 08 23:12	Cap Jan 05 05:23	Pis Feb 06 11:00
Aqu Dec 11 11:57	Aqu Jan 07 17:52	Ari Feb 08 19:16
Pis Dec 13 23:15	Pis Jan 10 04:58	Tau Feb 11 01:19

Gem Feb 13 05:22	Leo Mar 15 16:42	Lib Apr 16 07:35
Can Feb 15 07:44	Vir Mar 17 19:48	Sco Apr 18 14:35
Leo Feb 17 09:11	Lib Mar 19 23:57	Sag Apr 20 23:57
Vir Feb 19 10:53	Sco Mar 22 06:17	Cap Apr 23 11:46
Lib Feb 21 14:21	Sag Mar 24 15:42	Aqu Apr 26 00:40
Sco Feb 23 20:58	Cap Mar 27 03:50	Pis Apr 28 12:04
Sag Feb 26 07:09	Aqu Mar 29 16:33	Ari Apr 30 19:53
Cap Feb 28 19:44	Pis Apr 01 03:10	Tau May 02 23:52
Aqu Mar 02 08:13	Ari Apr 03 10:20	Gem May 05 01:22
Pis Mar 04 18:29	Tau Apr 05 14:27	Can May 07 02:13
Ari Mar 07 01:52	Gem Apr 07 16:57	Leo May 09 04:01
Tau Mar 09 07:00	Can Apr 09 19:15	Vir May 11 07:40
Gem Mar 11 10:44	Leo Apr 11 22:15	Lib May 13 13:27
Can Mar 13 13:50	Vir Apr 14 02:18	Sco May 15 21:16

Sag May 18 07:09 Aqu Jun 19 14:25 Ari Jul 21 19:08
Cap May 20 19:00 Pis Jun 22 02:50 Tau Jul 24 02:42
Aqu May 23 07:59 Ari Jun 24 12:53 Gem Jul 26 07:00
Pis May 25 20:06 Tau Jun 26 19:17 Can Jul 28 08:28
Ari May 28 05:06 Gem Jun 28 21:57 Leo Jul 30 08:23
Tau May 30 10:00 Can Jun 30 22:08 Vir Aug 01 08:27
Gem Jun 01 11:33 Leo Jul 02 21:37 Lib Aug 03 10:32
Can Jun 03 11:29 Vir Jul 04 22:19 Sco Aug 05 16:04
Leo Jun 05 11:45 Lib Jul 07 01:47 Sag Aug 08 01:30
Vir Jun 07 13:57 Sco Jul 09 08:48 Cap Aug 10 13:43
Lib Jun 09 18:58 Sag Jul 11 19:05 Aqu Aug 13 02:42
Sco Jun 12 02:55 Cap Jul 14 07:27 Pis Aug 15 14:40
Sag Jun 14 13:18 Aqu Jul 16 20:25 Ari Aug 18 00:42
Cap Jun 17 01:26 Pis Jul 19 08:42 Tau Aug 20 08:29

Gem Aug 22 13:53	Leo Sep 23 01:59	Lib Oct 24 14:29
Can Aug 24 16:58	Vir Sep 25 04:01	Sco Oct 26 19:23
Leo Aug 26 18:16	Lib Sep 27 06:21	Sag Oct 29 02:40
Vir Aug 28 18:54	Sco Sep 29 10:30	Cap Oct 31 13:01
Lib Aug 30 20:33	Sag Oct 01 17:49	Aqu Nov 03 01:39
Sco Sep 02 00:56	Cap Oct 04 04:42	Pis Nov 05 14:11
Sag Sep 04 09:08	Aqu Oct 06 17:32	Ari Nov 08 00:00
Cap Sep 06 20:46	Pis Oct 09 05:35	Tau Nov 10 06:11
Aqu Sep 09 09:43	Ari Oct 11 14:49	Gem Nov 12 09:26
Pis Sep 11 21:32	Tau Oct 13 21:04	Can Nov 14 11:20
Ari Sep 14 06:59	Gem Oct 16 01:17	Leo Nov 16 13:18
Tau Sep 16 14:04	Can Oct 18 04:36	Vir Nov 18 16:15
Gem Sep 18 19:21	Leo Oct 20 07:41	Lib Nov 20 20:34
Can Sep 20 23:14	Vir Oct 22 10:52	Sco Nov 23 02:32

Sag Nov 25 10:32
Cap Nov 27 20:56
Aqu Nov 30 09:25
Pis Dec 02 22:21
Ari Dec 05 09:15
Tau Dec 07 16:25
Gem Dec 09 19:49
Can Dec 11 20:47
Leo Dec 13 21:08
Vir Dec 15 22:30
Lib Dec 18 02:01
Sco Dec 20 08:11
Sag Dec 22 16:56
Cap Dec 25 03:53

Aqu Dec 27 16:24
Pis Dec 30 05:26

2001

Ari Jan 01 17:13
Tau Jan 04 01:54
Gem Jan 06 06:43
Can Jan 08 08:07
Leo Jan 10 07:43
Vir Jan 12 07:25
Lib Jan 14 09:05
Sco Jan 16 14:03
Sag Jan 18 22:36
Cap Jan 21 09:56

Aqu Jan 23 22:42
Pis Jan 26 11:37
Ari Jan 28 23:33
Tau Jan 31 09:19
Gem Feb 02 15:54
Can Feb 04 18:59
Leo Feb 06 19:20
Vir Feb 08 18:34
Lib Feb 10 18:45
Sco Feb 12 21:52
Sag Feb 15 05:02
Cap Feb 17 15:58
Aqu Feb 20 04:53
Pis Feb 22 17:44

Ari Feb 25 05:19	Gem Mar 29 04:00	Leo Apr 29 18:24
Tau Feb 27 15:04	Can Mar 31 09:21	Vir May 01 21:15
Gem Mar 01 22:34	Leo Apr 02 12:52	Lib May 03 23:49
Can Mar 04 03:23	Vir Apr 04 14:45	Sco May 06 03:00
Leo Mar 06 05:29	Lib Apr 06 15:56	Sag May 08 08:05
Vir Mar 08 05:43	Sco Apr 08 18:00	Cap May 10 16:09
Lib Mar 10 05:46	Sag Apr 10 22:47	Aqu May 13 03:19
Sco Mar 12 07:42	Cap Apr 13 07:20	Pis May 15 16:00
Sag Mar 14 13:17	Aqu Apr 15 19:10	Ari May 18 03:39
Cap Mar 16 23:02	Pis Apr 18 07:59	Tau May 20 12:27
Aqu Mar 19 11:35	Ari Apr 20 19:16	Gem May 22 18:11
Pis Mar 22 00:27	Tau Apr 23 03:54	Can May 24 21:41
Ari Mar 24 11:42	Gem Apr 25 10:10	Leo May 27 00:11
Tau Mar 26 20:49	Can Apr 27 14:48	Vir May 29 02:37

Lib May 31 05:40	Sag Jul 01 22:13	Aqu Aug 03 00:52
Sco Jun 02 09:56	Cap Jul 04 07:21	Pis Aug 05 13:29
Sag Jun 04 15:57	Aqu Jul 06 18:32	Ari Aug 08 02:03
Cap Jun 07 00:23	Pis Jul 09 07:04	Tau Aug 10 13:21
Aqu Jun 09 11:19	Ari Jul 11 19:34	Gem Aug 12 21:56
Pis Jun 11 23:52	Tau Jul 14 06:12	Can Aug 15 02:53
Ari Jun 14 12:01	Gem Jul 16 13:23	Leo Aug 17 04:24
Tau Jun 16 21:37	Can Jul 18 16:55	Vir Aug 19 03:52
Gem Jun 19 03:40	Leo Jul 20 17:42	Lib Aug 21 03:18
Can Jun 21 06:40	Vir Jul 22 17:28	Sco Aug 23 04:49
Leo Jun 23 07:54	Lib Jul 24 18:07	Sag Aug 25 09:59
Vir Jun 25 08:57	Sco Jul 26 21:17	Cap Aug 27 19:01
Lib Jun 27 11:10	Sag Jul 29 03:44	Aqu Aug 30 06:46
Sco Jun 29 15:28	Cap Jul 31 13:16	Pis Sep 01 19:31

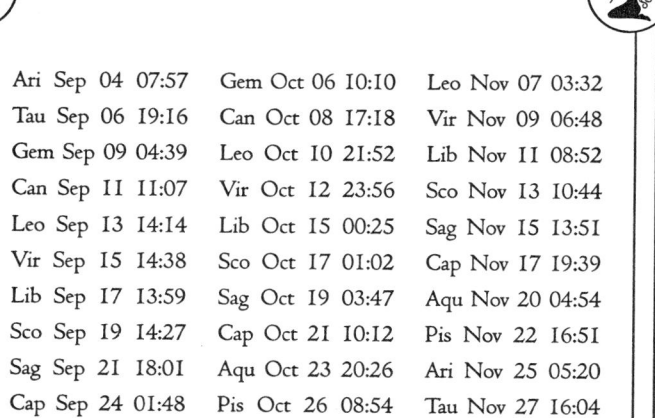

Ari Sep 04 07:57	Gem Oct 06 10:10	Leo Nov 07 03:32
Tau Sep 06 19:16	Can Oct 08 17:18	Vir Nov 09 06:48
Gem Sep 09 04:39	Leo Oct 10 21:52	Lib Nov 11 08:52
Can Sep 11 11:07	Vir Oct 12 23:56	Sco Nov 13 10:44
Leo Sep 13 14:14	Lib Oct 15 00:25	Sag Nov 15 13:51
Vir Sep 15 14:38	Sco Oct 17 01:02	Cap Nov 17 19:39
Lib Sep 17 13:59	Sag Oct 19 03:47	Aqu Nov 20 04:54
Sco Sep 19 14:27	Cap Oct 21 10:12	Pis Nov 22 16:51
Sag Sep 21 18:01	Aqu Oct 23 20:26	Ari Nov 25 05:20
Cap Sep 24 01:48	Pis Oct 26 08:54	Tau Nov 27 16:04
Aqu Sep 26 13:04	Ari Oct 28 21:13	Gem Nov 30 00:02
Pis Sep 29 01:49	Tau Oct 31 07:46	Can Dec 02 05:29
Ari Oct 01 14:06	Gem Nov 02 16:11	Leo Dec 04 09:14
Tau Oct 04 00:59	Can Nov 04 22:42	Vir Dec 06 12:10

Lib Dec 08 14:56	Lib Jan 04 20:23	Sag Feb 05 10:21
Sco Dec 10 18:08	Sco Jan 06 23:41	Cap Feb 07 18:07
Sag Dec 12 22:29	Sag Jan 09 04:57	Aqu Feb 10 04:14
Cap Dec 15 04:47	Cap Jan 11 12:18	Pis Feb 12 15:52
Aqu Dec 17 13:43	Aqu Jan 13 21:41	Ari Feb 15 04:24
Pis Dec 20 01:09	Pis Jan 16 08:59	Tau Feb 17 16:57
Ari Dec 22 13:44	Ari Jan 18 21:34	Gem Feb 20 03:48
Tau Dec 25 01:10	Tau Jan 21 09:45	Can Feb 22 11:13
Gem Dec 27 09:37	Gem Jan 23 19:26	Leo Feb 24 14:34
Can Dec 29 14:38	Can Jan 26 01:15	Vir Feb 26 14:45
Leo Dec 31 17:08	Leo Jan 28 03:29	Lib Feb 28 13:46
	Vir Jan 30 03:39	Sco Mar 02 13:52
2002	Lib Feb 01 03:44	Sag Mar 04 16:54
Vir Jan 02 18:33	Sco Feb 03 05:34	Cap Mar 06 23:48

Aqu Mar 09 09:56	Ari Apr 10 16:39	Gem May 12 22:03
Pis Mar 11 21:56	Tau Apr 13 04:54	Can May 15 06:32
Ari Mar 14 10:33	Gem Apr 15 15:55	Leo May 17 12:50
Tau Mar 16 22:59	Can Apr 18 00:59	Vir May 19 16:59
Gem Mar 19 10:18	Leo Apr 20 07:19	Lib May 21 19:17
Can Mar 21 19:05	Vir Apr 22 10:33	Sco May 23 20:37
Leo Mar 24 00:10	Lib Apr 24 11:20	Sag May 25 22:19
Vir Mar 26 01:42	Sco Apr 26 11:15	Cap May 28 01:54
Lib Mar 28 01:03	Sag Apr 28 12:13	Aqu May 30 08:34
Sco Mar 30 00:21	Cap Apr 30 16:02	Pis Jun 01 18:36
Sag Apr 01 01:49	Aqu May 02 23:44	Ari Jun 04 06:50
Cap Apr 03 06:58	Pis May 05 10:45	Tau Jun 06 19:05
Aqu Apr 05 16:06	Ari May 07 23:21	Gem Jun 09 05:28
Pis Apr 08 03:57	Tau May 10 11:30	Can Jun 11 13:13

Leo Jun 13 18:38	Lib Jul 15 06:38	Sag Aug 15 18:24
Vir Jun 15 22:22	Sco Jul 17 09:12	Cap Aug 18 00:15
Lib Jun 18 01:10	Sag Jul 19 13:02	Aqu Aug 20 08:16
Sco Jun 20 03:41	Cap Jul 21 18:25	Pis Aug 22 18:10
Sag Jun 22 06:41	Aqu Jul 24 01:39	Ari Aug 25 05:46
Cap Jun 24 11:01	Pis Jul 26 11:04	Tau Aug 27 18:30
Aqu Jun 26 17:35	Ari Jul 28 22:38	Gem Aug 30 06:44
Pis Jun 29 03:00	Tau Jul 31 11:15	Can Sep 01 16:12
Ari Jul 01 14:48	Gem Aug 02 22:44	Leo Sep 03 21:34
Tau Jul 04 03:15	Can Aug 05 07:00	Vir Sep 05 23:14
Gem Jul 06 13:58	Leo Aug 07 11:25	Lib Sep 07 22:56
Can Jul 08 21:34	Vir Aug 09 13:02	Sco Sep 09 22:48
Leo Jul 11 02:06	Lib Aug 11 13:37	Sag Sep 12 00:44
Vir Jul 13 04:39	Sco Aug 13 15:00	Cap Sep 14 05:47

Aqu Sep 16 13:54	Ari Oct 18 18:12	Gem Nov 20 01:23
Pis Sep 19 00:17	Tau Oct 21 06:55	Can Nov 22 11:46
Ari Sep 21 12:10	Gem Oct 23 19:16	Leo Nov 24 19:58
Tau Sep 24 00:53	Can Oct 26 06:09	Vir Nov 27 01:40
Gem Sep 26 13:25	Leo Oct 28 14:18	Lib Nov 29 04:53
Can Sep 28 23:59	Vir Oct 30 18:58	Sco Dec 01 06:14
Leo Oct 01 06:57	Lib Nov 01 20:27	Sag Dec 03 06:57
Vir Oct 03 09:50	Sco Nov 03 20:09	Cap Dec 05 08:38
Lib Oct 05 09:50	Sag Nov 05 20:01	Aqu Dec 07 12:54
Sco Oct 07 08:57	Cap Nov 07 21:59	Pis Dec 09 20:46
Sag Oct 09 09:21	Aqu Nov 10 03:27	Ari Dec 12 07:57
Cap Oct 11 12:45	Pis Nov 12 12:41	Tau Dec 14 20:42
Aqu Oct 13 19:51	Ari Nov 15 00:37	Gem Dec 17 08:41
Pis Oct 16 06:06	Tau Nov 17 13:22	Can Dec 19 18:29

Leo Dec 22 01:47
Vir Dec 24 07:04
Lib Dec 26 10:52
Sco Dec 28 13:40
Sag Dec 30 16:00

2003

Cap Jan 01 18:42
Aqu Jan 03 22:57
Pis Jan 06 05:56
Ari Jan 08 16:14
Tau Jan 11 04:47
Gem Jan 13 17:06
Can Jan 16 02:54

Leo Jan 18 09:27
Vir Jan 20 13:30
Lib Jan 22 16:22
Sco Jan 24 19:08
Sag Jan 26 22:25
Cap Jan 29 02:29
Aqu Jan 31 07:44
Pis Feb 02 14:54
Ari Feb 05 00:44
Tau Feb 07 12:58
Gem Feb 10 01:44
Can Feb 12 12:17
Leo Feb 14 19:03
Vir Feb 16 22:21

Lib Feb 18 23:47
Sco Feb 21 01:09
Sag Feb 23 03:45
Cap Feb 25 08:10
Aqu Feb 27 14:24
Pis Mar 01 22:25
Ari Mar 04 08:29
Tau Mar 06 20:35
Gem Mar 09 09:36
Can Mar 11 21:10
Leo Mar 14 05:05
Vir Mar 16 08:51
Lib Mar 18 09:42
Sco Mar 20 09:37

Sag Mar 22 10:33	Aqu Apr 23 01:58	Ari May 25 02:58
Cap Mar 24 13:48	Pis Apr 25 10:02	Tau May 27 15:31
Aqu Mar 26 19:50	Ari Apr 27 20:54	Gem May 30 04:30
Pis Mar 29 04:25	Tau Apr 30 09:25	Can Jun 01 16:26
Ari Mar 31 15:04	Gem May 02 22:26	Leo Jun 04 02:23
Tau Apr 03 03:19	Can May 05 10:40	Vir Jun 06 09:49
Gem Apr 05 16:23	Leo May 07 20:44	Lib Jun 08 14:28
Can Apr 08 04:35	Vir May 10 03:29	Sco Jun 10 16:37
Leo Apr 10 13:51	Lib May 12 06:41	Sag Jun 12 17:11
Vir Apr 12 19:05	Sco May 14 07:12	Cap Jun 14 17:37
Lib Apr 14 20:40	Sag May 16 06:42	Aqu Jun 16 19:41
Sco Apr 16 20:15	Cap May 18 07:03	Pis Jun 19 00:57
Sag Apr 18 19:51	Aqu May 20 10:01	Ari Jun 21 10:05
Cap Apr 20 21:20	Pis May 22 16:40	Tau Jun 23 22:14

Gem Jun 26 11:11	Leo Jul 28 15:15	Lib Aug 29 08:40
Can Jun 28 22:50	Vir Jul 30 21:25	Sco Aug 31 10:59
Leo Jul 01 08:12	Lib Aug 02 01:46	Sag Sep 02 13:31
Vir Jul 03 15:14	Sco Aug 04 05:11	Cap Sep 04 16:50
Lib Jul 05 20:19	Sag Aug 06 08:10	Aqu Sep 06 21:14
Sco Jul 07 23:42	Cap Aug 08 11:02	Pis Sep 09 03:06
Sag Jul 10 01:47	Aqu Aug 10 14:23	Ari Sep 11 11:09
Cap Jul 12 03:20	Pis Aug 12 19:18	Tau Sep 13 21:49
Aqu Jul 14 05:37	Ari Aug 15 03:00	Gem Sep 16 10:31
Pis Jul 16 10:14	Tau Aug 17 13:52	Can Sep 18 23:06
Ari Jul 18 18:18	Gem Aug 20 02:40	Leo Sep 21 09:01
Tau Jul 21 05:47	Can Aug 22 14:43	Vir Sep 23 15:02
Gem Jul 23 18:41	Leo Aug 24 23:46	Lib Sep 25 17:48
Can Jul 26 06:22	Vir Aug 27 05:25	Sco Sep 27 18:51

Sag Sep 29 19:56	Aqu Oct 31 08:41	Ari Dec 02 05:55
Cap Oct 01 22:21	Pis Nov 02 14:52	Tau Dec 04 17:29
Aqu Oct 04 02:45	Ari Nov 05 00:02	Gem Dec 07 06:25
Pis Oct 06 09:20	Tau Nov 07 11:28	Can Dec 09 19:10
Ari Oct 08 18:07	Gem Nov 10 00:13	Leo Dec 12 06:39
Tau Oct 11 05:04	Can Nov 12 13:09	Vir Dec 14 16:05
Gem Oct 13 17:44	Leo Nov 15 00:46	Lib Dec 16 22:44
Can Oct 16 06:40	Vir Nov 17 09:34	Sco Dec 19 02:18
Leo Oct 18 17:40	Lib Nov 19 14:40	Sag Dec 21 03:14
Vir Oct 21 00:59	Sco Nov 21 16:22	Cap Dec 23 02:55
Lib Oct 23 04:25	Sag Nov 23 16:02	Aqu Dec 25 03:13
Sco Oct 25 05:07	Cap Nov 25 15:31	Pis Dec 27 06:09
Sag Oct 27 04:54	Aqu Nov 27 16:48	Ari Dec 29 13:09
Cap Oct 29 05:36	Pis Nov 29 21:26	

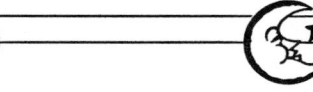

2004

	Gem Jan 30 20:17	Leo Mar 03 04:16
Tau Jan 01 00:01	Can Feb 02 09:02	Vir Mar 05 12:16
Gem Jan 03 12:57	Leo Feb 04 19:49	Lib Mar 07 17:30
Can Jan 06 01:37	Vir Feb 07 04:01	Sco Mar 09 21:02
Leo Jan 08 12:37	Lib Feb 09 10:11	Sag Mar 11 23:56
Vir Jan 10 21:36	Sco Feb 11 14:56	Cap Mar 14 02:51
Lib Jan 13 04:37	Sag Feb 13 18:34	Aqu Mar 16 06:09
Sco Jan 15 09:31	Cap Feb 15 21:13	Pis Mar 18 10:26
Sag Jan 17 12:16	Aqu Feb 17 23:27	Ari Mar 20 16:28
Cap Jan 19 13:23	Pis Feb 20 02:27	Tau Mar 23 01:09
Aqu Jan 21 14:10	Ari Feb 22 07:45	Gem Mar 25 12:34
Pis Jan 23 16:28	Tau Feb 24 16:30	Can Mar 28 01:22
Ari Jan 25 22:06	Gem Feb 27 04:22	Leo Mar 30 13:05
Tau Jan 28 07:46	Can Feb 29 17:11	Vir Apr 01 21:43

Lib Apr 04 02:50	Sag May 05 16:07	Aqu Jun 06 02:10
Sco Apr 06 05:23	Cap May 07 16:16	Pis Jun 08 04:38
Sag Apr 08 06:49	Aqu May 09 17:45	Ari Jun 10 10:50
Cap Apr 10 08:33	Pis May 11 21:52	Tau Jun 12 20:36
Aqu Apr 12 11:33	Ari May 14 05:02	Gem Jun 15 08:43
Pis Apr 14 16:23	Tau May 16 14:56	Can Jun 17 21:36
Ari Apr 16 23:24	Gem May 19 02:46	Leo Jun 20 10:03
Tau Apr 19 08:42	Can May 21 15:34	Vir Jun 22 21:08
Gem Apr 21 20:09	Leo May 24 04:06	Lib Jun 25 05:49
Can Apr 24 08:55	Vir May 26 14:50	Sco Jun 27 11:10
Leo Apr 26 21:13	Lib May 28 22:20	Sag Jun 29 13:14
Vir Apr 29 06:59	Sco May 31 02:06	Cap Jul 01 13:00
Lib May 01 13:00	Sag Jun 02 02:51	Aqu Jul 03 12:22
Sco May 03 15:37	Cap Jun 04 02:12	Pis Jul 05 13:27

Ari Jul 07 18:02	Gem Aug 08 21:32	Leo Sep 10 06:05
Tau Jul 10 02:50	Can Aug 11 10:19	Vir Sep 12 16:15
Gem Jul 12 14:44	Leo Aug 13 22:28	Lib Sep 14 23:52
Can Jul 15 03:40	Vir Aug 16 08:48	Sco Sep 17 05:24
Leo Jul 17 15:55	Lib Aug 18 17:08	Sag Sep 19 09:28
Vir Jul 20 02:43	Sco Aug 20 23:35	Cap Sep 21 12:34
Lib Jul 22 11:37	Sag Aug 23 04:07	Aqu Sep 23 15:09
Sco Jul 24 18:07	Cap Aug 25 06:46	Pis Sep 25 17:55
Sag Jul 26 21:46	Aqu Aug 27 08:07	Ari Sep 27 21:57
Cap Jul 28 22:56	Pis Aug 29 09:33	Tau Sep 30 04:23
Aqu Jul 30 22:54	Ari Aug 31 12:46	Gem Oct 02 13:55
Pis Aug 01 23:35	Tau Sep 02 19:15	Can Oct 05 01:53
Ari Aug 04 03:00	Gem Sep 05 05:24	Leo Oct 07 14:22
Tau Aug 06 10:26	Can Sep 07 17:49	Vir Oct 10 00:58

Lib Oct 12 08:30	Sag Nov 13 00:55	Aqu Dec 14 11:10
Sco Oct 14 13:09	Cap Nov 15 01:32	Pis Dec 16 12:24
Sag Oct 16 15:57	Aqu Nov 17 02:39	Ari Dec 18 16:52
Cap Oct 18 18:06	Pis Nov 19 05:37	Tau Dec 21 00:52
Aqu Oct 20 20:37	Ari Nov 21 11:11	Gem Dec 23 11:32
Pis Oct 23 00:13	Tau Nov 23 19:15	Can Dec 25 23:37
Ari Oct 25 05:24	Gem Nov 26 05:24	Leo Dec 28 12:13
Tau Oct 27 12:37	Can Nov 28 17:10	Vir Dec 31 00:32
Gem Oct 29 22:11	Leo Dec 01 05:49	
Can Nov 01 09:52	Vir Dec 03 17:59	**2005**
Leo Nov 03 22:31	Lib Dec 06 03:45	Lib Jan 02 11:18
Vir Nov 06 09:58	Sco Dec 08 09:41	Sco Jan 04 18:58
Lib Nov 08 18:22	Sag Dec 10 11:52	Sag Jan 06 22:42
Sco Nov 10 23:03	Cap Dec 12 11:41	Cap Jan 08 23:09

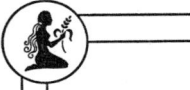

Aqu Jan 10 22:07	Ari Feb 11 10:22	Gem Mar 15 08:44
Pis Jan 12 21:51	Tau Feb 13 15:18	Can Mar 17 19:43
Ari Jan 15 00:27	Gem Feb 16 00:18	Leo Mar 20 08:16
Tau Jan 17 07:06	Can Feb 18 12:12	Vir Mar 22 20:09
Gem Jan 19 17:23	Leo Feb 21 00:53	Lib Mar 25 05:59
Can Jan 22 05:41	Vir Feb 23 12:43	Sco Mar 27 13:27
Leo Jan 24 18:20	Lib Feb 25 22:57	Sag Mar 29 18:55
Vir Jan 27 06:23	Sco Feb 28 07:19	Cap Mar 31 22:47
Lib Jan 29 17:12	Sag Mar 02 13:28	Aqu Apr 03 01:30
Sco Feb 01 01:49	Cap Mar 04 17:11	Pis Apr 05 03:45
Sag Feb 03 07:20	Aqu Mar 06 18:48	Ari Apr 07 06:27
Cap Feb 05 09:30	Pis Mar 08 19:32	Tau Apr 09 10:50
Aqu Feb 07 09:25	Ari Mar 10 21:03	Gem Apr 11 17:54
Pis Feb 09 08:59	Tau Mar 13 01:06	Can Apr 14 04:03

Leo Apr 16 16:16	Lib May 18 23:28	Sag Jun 19 20:43
Vir Apr 19 04:26	Sco May 21 06:47	Cap Jun 21 21:51
Lib Apr 21 14:25	Sag May 23 10:36	Aqu Jun 23 21:36
Sco Apr 23 21:24	Cap May 25 12:10	Pis Jun 25 22:03
Sag Apr 26 01:44	Aqu May 27 13:09	Ari Jun 28 00:52
Cap Apr 28 04:32	Pis May 29 15:09	Tau Jun 30 06:44
Aqu Apr 30 06:53	Ari May 31 19:07	Gem Jul 02 15:25
Pis May 02 09:42	Tau Jun 03 01:19	Can Jul 05 02:07
Ari May 04 13:36	Gem Jun 05 09:35	Leo Jul 07 14:10
Tau May 06 19:01	Can Jun 07 19:46	Vir Jul 10 02:56
Gem May 09 02:28	Leo Jun 10 07:39	Lib Jul 12 15:08
Can May 11 12:20	Vir Jun 12 20:21	Sco Jul 15 00:49
Leo May 14 00:16	Lib Jun 15 07:57	Sag Jul 17 06:34
Vir May 16 12:45	Sco Jun 17 16:22	Cap Jul 19 08:25

Aqu Jul 21 07:54	Ari Aug 21 18:00	Gem Sep 22 12:07
Pis Jul 23 07:11	Tau Aug 23 20:58	Can Sep 24 21:10
Ari Jul 25 08:23	Gem Aug 26 03:43	Leo Sep 27 09:02
Tau Jul 27 12:55	Can Aug 28 13:57	Vir Sep 29 21:43
Gem Jul 29 21:02	Leo Aug 31 02:14	Lib Oct 02 09:23
Can Aug 01 07:52	Vir Sep 02 14:55	Sco Oct 04 19:02
Leo Aug 03 20:09	Lib Sep 05 02:51	Sag Oct 07 02:27
Vir Aug 06 08:53	Sco Sep 07 13:09	Cap Oct 09 07:42
Lib Aug 08 21:07	Sag Sep 09 21:01	Aqu Oct 11 11:04
Sco Aug 11 07:33	Cap Sep 12 01:55	Pis Oct 13 13:04
Sag Aug 13 14:45	Aqu Sep 14 04:01	Ari Oct 15 14:39
Cap Aug 15 18:12	Pis Sep 16 04:24	Tau Oct 17 17:04
Aqu Aug 17 18:38	Ari Sep 18 04:42	Gem Oct 19 21:44
Pis Aug 19 17:52	Tau Sep 20 06:47	Can Oct 22 05:40

Leo Oct 24 16:48	Lib Nov 26 01:56	Sag Dec 28 03:42
Vir Oct 27 05:27	Sco Nov 28 11:31	Cap Dec 30 06:34
Lib Oct 29 17:14	Sag Nov 30 17:31	
Sco Nov 01 02:27	Cap Dec 02 20:41	
Sag Nov 03 08:54	Aqu Dec 04 22:36	
Cap Nov 05 13:16	Pis Dec 07 00:44	
Aqu Nov 07 16:30	Ari Dec 09 04:02	
Pis Nov 09 19:22	Tau Dec 11 08:46	
Ari Nov 11 22:22	Gem Dec 13 14:59	
Tau Nov 14 02:02	Can Dec 15 23:01	
Gem Nov 16 07:09	Leo Dec 18 09:18	
Can Nov 18 14:42	Vir Dec 20 21:38	
Leo Nov 21 01:10	Lib Dec 23 10:25	
Vir Nov 23 13:41	Sco Dec 25 21:02	

This book was

typeset in Centaur and KuenstlerScript
by Nina Gaskin.

Book design by

Judith Stagnitto Abbate and Junie Lee